SHAKEN & STIRRED

SHAKEN & STIRRED

THROUGH THE MARTINI GLASS
AND OTHER DRINKING ADVENTURES

WILLIAM L. HAMILTON

HarperResource
An Imprint of HarperCollins*Publishers*

FIRST EDITION

Designed by Eric Janssen Strohl, Eric Baker Design Associates

Library of Congress Cataloging-in-Publication Data

Hamilton, William L.
    Shaken and stirred : through the martini glass and other drinking adventures/
    William L. Hamilton
        p. cm.
    ISBN 0-06-074044-2
    1. Cocktails. 2. Drinking customs—Anecdotes. I. Title.

TX951.H224 2004
641.8'74—dc22   2004052373

04 05 06 07 08 ❖/RRD 10 9 8 7 6 5 4 3 2 1

FOR MY MOTHER AND FATHER

TABLE OF CONTENTS

"DRINK ME"

———————————◆———————————

— ALICE'S ADVENTURES IN WONDERLAND,
Lewis Carroll

ACKNOWLEDGMENTS

DRINKING ALONE'S NOT MUCH FUN. Even professionally. It has its uses, but avoid it when you can.

I want to thank my editors in the Style department at the *New York Times,* Luisita Lopez Torregrosa, Trip Gabriel and Barbara Graustark — perfect drinking companions from day one. And my editor at HarperResource, Kathryn Huck, for her enthusiasm and patience, and her "mixologist's" skill and sense of balance in keeping me on the right and good side of wrong and bad decisions in publishing a book.

Also, my thanks to David McCormick, for translating intentions into deeds, with empathetic efficiency.

And my thanks to my "Drinks of Mass Destruction" inspection team. You know who you are. Also, my thanks to the bartenders, cocktail creators, chefs, bar staff, aficionados and aficionadas who generously shared their knowledge, over a drink, in a letter or over the telephone.

And lastly, my thanks to Richard "Mojito" Fox, who taught me measure in all things. If you're going to drink of life, take it one well-deserved drink at a time.

INTRODUCTION

DRINKING ON THE JOB

I DRANK MY FIRST COCKTAIL WHEN I WAS SIX, in the mid-twentieth century, when martinis were sacramental, and the cocktail hour, or the "violet hour," as Ian Fleming calls it in one of the James Bond novels, was a moment of prayer, poised like a thin chilled glass to the lips between the mortal pressures of the day and the infinity of night.

The cocktail was a ritual that included even children. My preference at six—a "boyhattan." Hold the whiskey, extra cherry. Who knew it was an early career move?

My next mixed drink was the gimlet, discovered in the heatwave of the summer of 1986. Ice cold when it's right, it kept me as cool as the big BTUs, but it ruined my reputation for thinking before I speak. I accept the trade-off. And I still badger bartenders to make the gimlet as close to frozen as they can, because you want the liquid to go down as though it were the purest excitement. Which it is.

There's a terrific amount of interest in cocktails right now. Acknowledging that, the *New York Times* started a regular column on cocktails, "Shaken and Stirred," in April 2002, in the Sunday Styles section. I report and write it.

Why cocktails? Why now? Probably a couple of reasons. They've had their heydays before, in the late nineteenth century, the early twentieth century, mid-century, and with the retrospective revivals of the 1980s and 1990s, when lounge culture and cocktail culture synonymously changed the way many people socialized. Cocktail drinking became a young, urban style of life unto itself—a martini culture that transcended gin and vermouth.

But this round is different. Among other things, the cocktail has become an issue of connoisseurship and identity, well beyond the brand of gin or vodka or Scotch you buy or the bar you drink it at. Or whether you like your drink shaken or stirred.

The moment has new gravitas, if that is not antithetical to the idea of drinking. It has less to do with the self-conscious cocktail and lounge scene of the late last century—the tiki bars and the cigar bars and the cosmopolitan's sexual politics—than with the silver age of the 1920s, when a cocktail was emblematic of modernity and invention, liberty and license to be original. Drinking one in the bar you liked best or serving your favorite at home was a way not only of socializing stylishly but of showing people who you were. It was not a fad or an affectation or a broad wink. It was a singular and impeccable pronunciation of character.

The cocktail, as it is again today, was also a quintessential luxury good, widely understood as such and accessible to most—a piece of the high life that anyone could swing through the air like a ring on the finger, the water that ran out of the taps "at the top." And for all its artifice, it was as natural as having a laugh, or taking a drink.

The martini glass was as strong an icon in the 1920s as the automobile or the smart-set Hollywood of the "Thin Man" series, where even the dog drank. And it is as strong an icon today of a worldly knowledge—or its ambition—as any of the international brands that drive the market for luxury. No matter what kind of drink you put in it. The martini glass's panoptic shape is as recognizable as the locked initials on a belt or a handbag.

In this last two years of drinking, in what I would argue is a new, golden era of interest in cocktails, there are several things that make it a real and not an imagined arrival.

The twelve-dollar cocktail. And up. I know. By the time you read this, that's going to seem quaint, and your first question will be: "Where can I find one?" But when the cocktail broke the ten-dollar barrier and continued to climb as bars, lounges and restaurants started to reinvent and sell it as a specialty item—the house deluxe—and not just a drink, the cocktail took on a life of its own.

It became the artistic work of a "bar chef," not a bartender, or a signature from a four-star kitchen, or the label-wearing liquid of a roster of rare ingredients, or the summation of an establishment's scene—a piece of potable fashion.

And it was no longer an issue of reviving the classics, though they held strong. The martini is unlikely to be dethroned. But it was joined on the dais by the cosmopolitan, what one observer, Nicole Beland, called the "girlie" martini, in deference to its popularity with the single women of *Sex and the City*, the HBO television show, and "Sex's" national Sunday-nightly sisterhood.

The revivals gained a second wind as younger drinkers discovered classics like the sidecar and the French 75 and the Cuban mojito. And the martini multiplied into unrecognizability: "tini" became as familiar a suffix to the newest generation of drinkers as ".com." And cocktail Websites, like *The Great Plate* or *Drinkboy* or *Cocktail Times,* were suddenly as ubiquitous as bars.

In addition to new bars, lounges and restaurants, parties and press events routinely served specially created cocktails, and cocktail conception specialists like Jerri Banks, Francesco Lafranconi and Dushan Zaric and Jason Kosmas of Cocktail Conceptions are now an established part of the liquor industry.

With a willingness to experiment, true originality appeared. Many of the newest cocktails were not just novel, but investigative and intelligent, and indicative of a larger scope of changing tastes. If one clear horizon emerged on my watch, it was the cocktail's crossover into cooking's global interests in "fusion." Fusion drinks, especially cocktails with an Asian influence, ruled specialty bar menus in much of New York for many months.

And the bartender's vocabulary of ingredients widened substantially as Asian spirits like sake and shochu became bases for creating cocktails, and fruits and herbs like calamansi and shiso were employed as juices and embellishments. Even the martini met its match, with variations like the Bo Hai, a sophisticatedly subtle "sake-tini" served at Riingo, an American Japanese restaurant opened by a celebrated New York chef, Marcus Samuelsson (himself an Ethiopian Swede).

Inventiveness arrived at a price. And ordering from the lists of new cocktails was the tip of an economic iceberg. The liquor industry, fueled by vodka, jumped on the wagon with a record number of flavored spirit introductions, to capitalize on the curiosity about unusual tastes, and upped the ante on the fuel grades. Gin, rum, Cognac, tequila and others are following suit. Premium vodkas shifted gear into "super-premiums," then "ultra-premiums," pushing the purchase of a cocktail or a 750 milliliter bottle into an act that came closer to being a downpayment on a style of life than a chance to enjoy a drink. Frank Gehry, the architect, designed a vodka bottle in 2004 for Wyborowa, a Polish ultra-premium.

Cocktail drinking in the last two years also coincided with a desire, perhaps generational, to socialize more simply, or more casually. In part, it accommodated attractively a downturn in the economy. A twelve-dollar cocktail in the best restaurant, at the nicest hotel, or in the most exclusive club was a comfortable cry from a hundred-dollar meal or a five-hundred-dollar room, but it was still an authentic part of the action.

Restaurants in particular responded in kind, increasing their emphasis—with expanding floor space and atmospheric amenity— on bar areas and people who came for cocktails, not dining. As Danny Meyer, the popular New York restaurateur who opened Union Square Cafe in 1985, said of the current situation, "It's a cocktail generation. It's fun, it's sexy. It's more fun than a glass of Chardonnay." Fifty percent of the customers at Blue Smoke, Mr. Meyer's newest restaurant and bar, were there to drink, not to dine, he said.

Food and decoration and design magazines encouraged the same kind of entertaining at home, with cocktail party–planning features. And upscale furnishing businesses like Pottery Barn, Crate and Barrel and Williams-Sonoma equipped the cocktail customer with expanding selections of barware and home bar accessories. To that end, the fine-food industry also moved to capture its corner of the market with introductions of specialty items like unusual martini olives and cocktail onions. There are currently more than five hundred producers of specialty garnishes in the United States, up from a handful in the 1980s.

The interest, economics and changing tastes together indicated the most important phenomenon, which pushed cocktails into center stage—the acceptance by women of cocktail drinking as a social form, and a new equality of enjoyment in going out. The cocktail scene, as opposed to the bar scene, was sexually comfortable and independent—mutually neutral territory where a group of any description could spend a few hours or an evening over a few conversation-piece drinks or a few favorites.

The industry acknowledged women quickly as a market force, as cocktail-compatible spirits like vodka and flavored vodkas led liquor sales to the detriment of the brown barroom standards like whiskey, and bars and lounges became as design-conscious as boutiques, or as visibly unconcerned with gender issues as a co-ed college dormitory.

This is history, and I've tried to keep it that way. Time references such as "Wednesday night" and "last week" as recorded for the *NYT* columns reappearing here, are moments in time, ringing with excited voices like a crowd in a bar: part remembrance, part reflection on the future to come. It keeps a drink fresh. Hopefully, in this book, you will find what I found, like the ingredients of a great cocktail: the high and the low life, the men and women, the new and the old, the sad and the sweet, and the arguments, like unbreakable friendships, that never die. Thirst, sex, adulthood, childhood, Champagne, vodka, gin, Hpnotiq, Dr. Brown's Cream Soda. Mix it any way you like.

And me? I'm just here to drink. This is a drinker's guide to drinking—cocktails and the people who love them, the people who make them, the people who invent them and the people who push the buttons behind the scene, from hip-hop musicians, who can elevate a brand's recognition like a high-five, to industry figures like Michel Roux of Absolut vodka, who decided that gin's problem was that it wasn't blue. He's trying to fix that. If you want to know how to make the perfect martini, ask John Conti (page 163), not me. He knows.

When I lift my gimlet for that first taste, and admire its color—a pale crystal green, like a legendary jewel—I'm reminded of Lewis Carroll's Alice and her healthy sense of adventure. When confronted with a bottle with a label that instructed her to down it, she did: "Alice ventured to taste it, and finding it very nice (it had, in fact, a sort of mixed flavour of cherry-tart, custard, pine-apple, roast turkey, toffee, and hot buttered toast), she very soon finished it off."

In today's world, it would be a Wondertini. Alice, you'd be fun to go drinking with.

CHAMPAGNE LIFE

THERE ARE NIGHTS WHEN YOU THINK
YOU'LL NEVER DRINK AGAIN

Sparkling Mango

DUSHAN ZARIC HAS, TO MY MIND, a unique and concise view of life.

"You like it sweet? You like sour?" he asked me last week. "You like bitter? You like dirty? Straight?"

I thought about all that, maybe a little too deeply.

Mr. Zaric is a bartender, and we were talking about cocktails. He is also, with Jason Kosmas, a fellow bartender, a partner in Cocktail Conceptions, a consulting service in Astoria, Queens, in the apartment the two men share and where they develop cocktails for restaurants, bars and liquor companies. They have been friends for four years and have a combined bartending experience of thirteen years.

"You have to be behind the bar," Mr. Zaric said. "If you're not behind the bar, you're going to lose touch with your basics."

Cocktail Conceptions, which is actually Mr. Zaric and Mr. Kosmas's dining room table, set up with liquors, barware and glassware, jars of sugars and vanilla beans, homemade infusions and bowls of fruits currently in the markets in Astoria, has worked for Courvoisier, Beefeater, Mumm and Perrier Jouët Champagne, and the new Stoli Premier.

One of Cocktail Conceptions' latest assignments was the cocktail menu at Schiller's Liquor Bar. It is Keith McNally's newest venture, at the corner of Rivington and Norfolk Streets. The white neon sign makes it look, cleverly, like an all-night pharmacy in a bad neighborhood.

There was a point in time when it might have been brilliant to put Mr. McNally on the City Planning Commission. He invaded and occupied frontier territories like TriBeCa with the restaurant Odeon in 1980 and eastern SoHo with Pravda in 1996 and Balthazar in 1997. Mr. McNally's recent posts are more like cleanup missions in well-publicized locales: Pastis in the meatpacking district in 1999 and Schiller's, opened last month, on the Lower East Side.

Mr. McNally asked Mr. Zaric, who also works at the bar, for frozen margaritas and then cut him loose to invent the house drinks.

"I didn't want us to appear too fancy, but to bring it down a little—not just cocktails," Mr. McNally said. "And I like them. But, I've got quite bad taste."

In Astoria, the request sent a freezing chill down the spines of Mr. Zaric and Mr. Kosmas, like the time Mr. Kosmas saw a maraschino cherry in a cosmopolitan.

"I threw away a lot of it," Mr. Zaric said of their research, conducted at the dining table beneath a portrait of Tito, the president of the former Yugoslavia. (Mr. Zaric is from Belgrade.)

"It's a sentimental, not an ideological thing," Mr. Zaric said, referring to Tito. "The guy was a great scamster. We have respect for that."

How do they start, in inventing a cocktail?

"Shopping," Mr. Zaric said.

"Shopping," Mr. Kosmas agreed. "On 30th Avenue here, there's a whole bunch of produce markets—everything you can imagine." On the dining table were white peaches, green apples, crabapples and pomegranates.

"I juiced ten cases of those once," Mr. Kosmas said, gesturing toward the pomegranates. "I had a white apron on. I looked like a butcher."

At Schiller's on Wednesday, it was business as usual—Mr. McNally's standard bistro background and, in the crowd, Europeans in track suits, artists with children and couples who probably weren't of age when Mr. McNally opened his last restaurant. There were also older men in short-sleeved polyester shirts—the aging aristocracy of the East Village and the Lower East Side.

If Schiller's frozen margaritas are an honorable escape, the Sparkling Mango is a triumph. There are nights when you think you'll never drink again, and then you come upon a drink like it, a piece of exoticism whose simplicity is its surprise.

"You get this sweet-and-sour kind of thing, but then, you get the bubbles," Mr. Zaric said proudly.

Consider it the newest of life's choices.

SPARKLING MANGO

ADAPTED FROM SCHILLER'S LIQUOR BAR

$^3/_4$ ounce 80 proof vodka
$^3/_4$ ounce Hiram Walker Fruja Mango
$^1/_2$ ounce fresh lemon juice
Chilled Champagne or sparkling water
Thin slice fresh mango

Pour all the liquid ingredients except the Champagne into a mixing glass. Add ice. Shake well for several seconds. Strain into a chilled 5-ounce martini glass and top to the brim with Champagne. Garnish with a mango slice.

Yield: 1 serving

MAKE YOUR LIFE FALL AWAY

French 75

THERE ISN'T GOLD AT THE END OF THE RAINBOW in New York. There's a seventeen-dollar cocktail. On Monday night, I went up to the Rainbow Grill, on the sixty-fifth floor of Rockefeller Center—what's left of the Promenade Bar, which originally accompanied the Rainbow Room, once the city's most famous supper club. I was looking for a French 75.

The French 75 is a classic cocktail, *circa* World War I, which is currently regaining recognition. It is named for the French 75-millimeter gun used by Allied troops, including, according to one story, Captain Harry S Truman. The drink's munitions are Cognac and Champagne. The simplest recipe calls for little more than a twist of lemon. Versions that take prisoners include liqueurs.

The Ciprianis, the Venetian restaurateurs, operate the Rainbow complex now, and they have taken a lot of heat for the way they maintain one of the greatest legends of New York night life. The Rainbow Grill, with its cafeteria sense of style, is a tourist-class accommodation of the former Promenade Bar—an Italian ferry of a certain age, with an observation deck where the swank and the swell once held sway. Of course, Manhattan at night from the top of Midtown is still a black ocean of magic, wired with stars. And no one can pull the plug on that.

I was prepared for a cynical experience, until Sharif Nagaiya, the bartender, took my order.

"Can you make a French 75?" I asked.

"Yes, sir," Mr. Nagaiya answered, and set to work with the kind of methodical second nature that you don't acquire unless you've tended bar a long, long time and know every drink—and every type of customer—in the book. He has worked with the Rainbow for fifteen years.

Mr. Nagaiya, an engaging Ghanaian who looked as though he was fat as a child, teased for it, and had compensated beautifully, set the French 75 in front of me and left me to take a sip. Like the best bartenders, he let the drink speak for itself.

The French 75 is a handsome cinnamon suede color, and its taste, as mixed by Mr. Nagaiya, has a cinnamon tone, too. When I admired it, Mr. Nagaiya took his place of pride beside the drink.

"I make the best," he said, adding, in an open challenge, "I like competition."

The cocktail is clearly of a previous era, with an emphasis on luxury items like Cognac and Champagne, and is unusual in a genteel way: no dishonorable tricks.

To share it with a view that was created in 1934 and that has become more dynamic with every year is to understand what a modern idea the cocktail was. Exhausted by present-day pressures, New York looks young again from the Rainbow's bar, in the same way that a well-made cocktail can make your life fall away behind you and leave you with only the future glittering in your eye.

That could be worth any price.

FRENCH 75

2 ounces Cognac
1 ounce maraschino liqueur
1 ounce Cointreau
Dash of fresh lemon juice
Orange twist
1 ounce Champagne

Shake all the ingredients, except the Champagne, in a tall shaker filled with ice. Strain and pour into a cold martini glass. Top to the brim with Champagne. Garnish with flamed orange twist. (Hold a lighted match briefly to the twist to release its oil.)

Yield: 1 serving

A'IGHBALL

Raspberry Caipiruska & French Mojito

A NEW COCKTAIL FROM PARIS, JUST LIKE THE OLD DAYS. In the 1920s, when expatriate Americans overran Paris, Americans drank cocktails, and Parisian bartenders at places like Harry's New York Bar or the bar at the Ritz Paris served them. They invented standards like the bloody mary and the sidecar. And most of the most popular drinks took the transatlantic trip back.

Now, Mix, the modern French American restaurant that opened in September as a partnership between Jeffrey Chodorow, the club restaurateur behind scene-setters like China Grill and Asia de Cuba, and Alain Ducasse, the chef with eight Michelin stars, is serving a house cocktail called the French Mojito. It could give the original a run for its money.

Mix, it appears, wanted nothing less than a signature drink. When you've got more stars than a movie, you don't rest on how many cosmopolitans you sell, I'm guessing. The restaurant's bar, which employed Thierry Hernandez, and now Xavier Herit, from the Hotel Plaza Athénée in Paris, tried a truffle martini—truffle juice sprayed onto the glass in place of vermouth, with orange vodka. For an idea so potent, it was a nondescript drink. The truffles used were

Chinese, not French, and inferior, and the cocktail was more power of suggestion than sensation—a dimly dirty-tasting snore. (If you try this at home, use French or Italian truffles and garnish with a slice of truffle, not a lemon twist, as Mix did. You'll hit real pay dirt instead, in both senses of the words.)

Mr. Herit is currently experimenting with raspberries, muddled and pureed, for a raspberry caipiruska, which will be introduced shortly on the spring and summer menu. A caipiruska is a vodka caipirinha.

On Friday, Mr. Herit, a proud young man who looked like a French military academy cadet, dressed in a black shirt and black trousers with a black belt and silver buckle, called it a " 'ighball" as he served the caipiruska on ice with two fat straws.

"You are the first customer," he explained, waiting for the test results to post. The drink is refreshing, if slight, and big on raspberry. There is raspberry-flavored vodka in it, too.

"Something that doesn't break you at the beginning of the night," Mr. Herit said, acknowledging that pacing is as an important part of cocktail drinking as anything else.

Mix, designed by Patrick Jouin, who is Mr. Ducasse's design doppelganger right now, is weirdly contemporary, like French pop music—you're never sure whether it's stylish or silly. White brick walls are encased in plate glass, the kind of chic architectural display you see in museums in France. The gray upholstered furniture is blenderized Arne Jacobsen and Eero Saarinen. The plate settings are white with orange Creamsicle centers. The bar area, called "The Tunnel," is a tube of space with a black ceiling, what the maître d'hôtel explained was "liquid-leather," with abstracted maps of America and Europe superimposed in white. Mix is marked with a red X, like a bombing target, or the place to dig for treasure.

The French Mojito was served initially at the Hotel Plaza Athénée, and Mr. Ducasse and his team have brought the new mojito with them to New York. It very simply substitutes Champagne for club soda, and it works, to brilliant effect.

You might think that the cocktail is an American drink. But Paris hasn't lost its touch.

RASPBERRY CAIPIRUSKA

ADAPTED FROM MIX

6 fresh raspberries
$^3/_4$ ounce raspberry puree *(available in most fine-food stores)*
1 tablespoon raw sugar
1 tablespoon simple syrup *(1 part superfine sugar to 1 part water;
shake or stir to dissolve sugar)*
2 ounces Stoli Razberi
Fresh sprig mint

Muddle the fresh raspberries together with the raspberry puree, raw sugar and syrup in a rocks glass or old-fashioned lowball glass. Fill to the rim with crushed ice. Top with vodka and garnish with fresh mint.

Yield: 1 serving

FRENCH MOJITO

ADAPTED FROM MIX

8 fresh sprigs mint
2 tablespoons raw sugar
1 tablespoon fresh lime juice
1 tablespoon simple syrup
2 ounces light rum
Champagne
Lime slice

Muddle the mint (save one sprig), sugar, lime juice and simple syrup together in a highball glass and fill to the rim with ice. Add rum, then top with Champagne. Garnish with a sprig of mint and slice of lime.

Yield: 1 serving

A CHAMPAGNE SNOW GLOBE

Champagne Cocktail

TRYING TO COME UP WITH A DRINK TO SERVE that's the holidays in a glass is a tall order.

I've never been sold on eggnog, to me a nauseating idea from its name on down to the nutmeg. The fact that you can buy it in supermarkets, in dairy cases, like a quart of brunch omelets, doesn't help.

But Champagne—what's not to like a lot? It pops; it bubbles; it knows how to work a glass. It acts like a party guest. And Champagne cocktails can be an improvement on the drink, which is strangely banal after a flute or two, like beauty without any social backup.

A midpriced bottle of Champagne or a similar sparkling wine, eighteen dollars or so, is a useful economy, too, served as kir royales, with the addition of a fruit liqueur like crème de cassis or crème de framboise. You can look for less likely, more exotic flavors, like crème de pêche, which is peach, or crème de mûre, blackberry. It's a nice touch to have a bar stocked with an interesting variety. With white wine, they make a good rotation of aperitifs year-round.

The standard Champagne cocktail is Champagne poured over a sugar cube soaked in Angostura bitters. The drink dates back to the nineteenth century and had a heyday in the 1930s. A variant with Cognac was called the Gloria Swanson in the late 1940s, shortly before she played Norma Desmond in *Sunset Boulevard*. The drink, besides being Ms. Swanson's calling card, was also known in other circles as the king's ruin, named for the society café and hotel bar habits of deposed European royalty. You feel lightheaded without the crown anyway—why not drink all day?

The diamond fizz is Champagne with the juice of a lemon and a teaspoon of sugar. The black velvet adds Guinness stout. My favorite, the stratosphere (who wouldn't try it to find out?), calls for crème Yvette, which is produced from Parma violets and turns out a purple cocktail. You garnish it with cloves.

And there's the Bellini, with prosecco, an Italian sparkling wine.

At Craft, Tom Colicchio's ingredient-fanatical restaurant at 43 East 19th Street in New York, the house drink is a Champagne cocktail that is seasonal like the food.

During the fall and winter, Matthew MacCartney, the beverage director, mixes Champagne with cubes of Bartlett pear bathed briefly in a pear liqueur. The taste, as simple as something perfectly ripe, is fresher than the sum of its parts.

"You don't want to overcomplicate it," Mr. MacCartney said. "You don't want to cover up its taste. Adding pear gives the drink an extra subtlety, more aroma, and it's pleasing to the eye."

Craft claims that if you make the cocktail correctly, the pear will "dance" in the glass.

It's a Champagne snow globe. For a holiday drink, how much happier can you get?

CHAMPAGNE COCKTAIL

ADAPTED FROM CRAFT

1 fresh Bartlett pear
About 1 cup pear liqueur *(Craft uses Belle de Brillet)*
5 ounces Champagne

Peel, seed and dice the pear into uniform $\frac{1}{4}$-inch cubes. Place the cubes in a plastic container and pour in enough pear liqueur to cover. Let the pear macerate in the refrigerator for 2 hours (not more, or the cubes will become oversaturated). If the pear is properly macerated, the cubes will dance in the glass.

When ready to serve, spoon about 1 teaspoon of macerated pear into the bottom of a Champagne flute. Pour Champagne slowly into the flute (Craft uses a Riedel Restaurant Series glass, with more of a wineglass shape), because it tends to bubble up in reaction to the pears. Serve.

Yield: 1 serving

A RECIPE FOR A PERFECT DAY

The Snack Bar Pitcher

SNACK BAR, A RESTAURANT AND BAR OPENING AT 111 West 17th Street tomorrow, has a novel four-step approach to serving cocktails—you order any drink on the menu in a shot, martini, highball, or pitcher size.

This makes Snack Bar feel more like it's operating a water authority than a bar. (They might have to do meter readings past a certain hour.)

It also raises a quick question. With Memorial Day here and the start of summer holidays hitting the blood like alcohol, who would order a 2-ounce shot and suffer the wait for the next one? Ask the bartender to set down a 32-ounce pitcher of the house cocktail—lemon vodka, crème de framboise, fresh grapefruit and raspberries, numb with ice—and decide one leisurely drink later who, or how many, to share it with. Let the pitcher do the sweating, and chill.

The house cocktail—known as the Snack Bar—was developed by Krim Boughalem, an owner, who was once a waiter at Bouley and bar manager at Daniel. Mr. Boughalem opened and sold Boughalem, a bistro on Bedford Street. Snack Bar is his new venture, with Nick Tischler, a chef with whom he worked at Bouley.

With its black concrete bar, parchment paper sconces and walls of grass cloth and glazed tile, the place has the kind of relaxed ambience that (like your average New Yorker out on the town in the summer) never loses sight of the fact that every encounter is an appearance. That crisp open-neck, tail-out shirt isn't an accident of birth. It's Bergdorf Goodman Men.

Mr. Boughalem, whose hair brushes his collar, understands how to be casual without forfeiting the formalities that make a drink a cocktail and not a glass of punch. The Snack Bar's vodka, with a light twist of the taste of lemon (the restaurant infuses its own in a big picnic jar at the bar), strikes tart to grapefruit's sweeter acidity. Crème de framboise, a raspberry liqueur, is soured slightly by a mash of fresh raspberries. This is science, not kids in the kitchen.

"I love citruses and raspberries," Mr. Boughalem said on Thursday, as though they were a recipe for a perfect day. Mr. Boughalem's three-year-old daughter, Isabella, paced the bar, pulling juice through a built-in straw in a plastic lidded cup, as though she and not her father were trying to get a new restaurant open in the next three days.

The Snack Bar has sparkling wine in it, too, to make it lively, a little conversational. The bar uses Vin du Bugey Cerdon, a rosé. Mr. Boughalem recommended also trying any effervescent white, including Champagne.

Snack Bar garnishes the pitcher with a slice of grapefruit, like a Mediterranean sun. You might drink until it goes down in the evening: the house cocktail isn't wearing a watch, and it's as sensual as tropical weather.

It's also a color you would pay a lot for in a summer shirt.

THE SNACK BAR PITCHER

ADAPTED FROM SNACK BAR

10 fresh raspberries
4 ounces lemon vodka
1 ounce crème de framboise
8 ounces fresh grapefruit juice *(save a slice of grapefruit as garnish)*
8 ounces Champagne, sparkling white wine or sparkling rosé
(Vin du Bugey or a Loire Valley sparkling wine)

Fill a pitcher (at least 32 ounces) with ice cubes. Crush the raspberries in a bowl; mix with vodka and crème de framboise. Separately, mix grapefruit juice with Champagne. Add both mixtures to the pitcher and garnish with the grapefruit slice.

Yield: 4 servings

AND YES, IT'S REALLY NANCY DREW

Titanic

In this column, published in 2003, Kimberly Sevy is speaking of the effects of September 11, 2001, and the attack on the World Trade Center in New York. The trend of meeting for cocktails, and of restaurants emphasizing drink menus and casual dining, has only increased since. Citarella became Josephs in April 2004.

AT SEVEN P.M. ON WEDNESDAY IN MIDTOWN, what most interested Ven Medabalmi about Citarella—the $3 million restaurant designed by the celebrity architect David Rockwell and boasting a David Bouley–trained chef, Brian Bistrong, in its kitchen— was the twelve-dollar cocktail he was drinking.

Mr. Medabalmi, twenty-eight, who had arrived with two friends, bumped into another friend, who was there with two companions; they were now a party of six. None of them was headed upstairs to the acclaimed dining room.

"I'll grab something later in my neighborhood, something local, something quick," said Mr. Medabalmi, a lawyer, wearing a suit with a dark dress shirt and without a necktie. "I've found that recently, people are not as inclined to go out to eat. Every time you propose dinner, people are like, 'Well, we'll just meet for a drink.' It's less complicated, less logistics. And you can do it more often during a week."

Mr. Medabalmi said that he chose Citarella's bar because "the atmosphere is clearly nicer" than a standard bar, and "the drinks are more interesting." (The house's most popular specialty cocktail is the Titanic, with a Champagne "iceberg." Cold and crisp as sea air at night. You don't hit it—it hits you.)

Kimberly Sevy, a friend of Mr. Medabalmi who had one denimed leg tucked under her as she sat at the bar, agreed.

"It's very mellow," said Ms. Sevy, a waitress who is also twenty-eight. "You have a chance to relax and have a cocktail and be able to have a conversation with people and not scream. Times have changed. We've all gone through something. The economy's not so fabulous, and anyone who lived in New York in the last year went through incredible trauma. When I go out, I just want to spend time with the people I'm with and talk." Yes, Ms. Sevy conceded, "this is a big change for me."

The cocktail's renaissance as a sophisticated way to drink has coincided with a cultural moment—a hunger for the comforts of casual behavior. Underscored by the economic moment, which is bad, meeting for drinks has produced a new version of the old night out—not the prelude to the evening, but the main event.

It is not about barhopping, with its mating and dating, or the power and prestige of a nine o'clock table at the best new restaurant—sacred cattle of New York City.

It is, instead, an easier, cheaper, friendlier alternative, increasingly popular—a last-minute plan with lower stakes, higher flexibility, a maximum of social entertainment in a minimum of time and a sweet lack of stress.

The taste for cocktails, a shaky pocket and an impatience with self-imposed pressures in the face of real threats are telling many people something that they might have suspected but not yet admitted.

They want the night off when they go out for the night.

"This is not about getting blunted," said Cyndi Stivers, editorial director of *Time Out New York,* the weekly listings magazine, which is publishing a pocket guidebook to bars on May 23 because, she said, "bars are all anybody goes to."

"Dinner's so intimate," she said. "Bars have a less serious veneer. People are going out in groups now, even on dates, and keeping things casual."

Bars introduced an effective concept, the lounge, years ago, with club-style seating and suave lighting for drinkers who wanted mood with their martinis. But restaurants, experts at ambience that were likened to theater in the 1980s and 1990s, are facing what E. Charles Hunt, the executive vice president of the New York State Restaurant Association, called "the perfect storm"—a fatal confluence of 9/11, the war in Iraq and the economy. Fewer people want to be onstage for two hours, eat three courses and pay four figures.

"I've never seen anything like it," he said of the circumstances hovering over the higher end of an industry that now wants a larger piece of the new cocktail bar action.

Mr. Hunt said that savvy restaurateurs are adapting to the strongest areas of the market. "Hopefully, you'll stay for dinner," he said. "But if you have a drink or finger food and move on—God love you, you're in the chair. The toughest thing in the world in a restaurant is an empty chair."

The average price of a meal at New York restaurants dropped last year for the first time since 1990, said Tim Zagat, a founder of the Zagat Survey and guides. He attributed the decline in part to people's eating less formally, or "bar style" as he called it, ordering smaller, appetizer-size plates.

Citarella, on Avenue of the Americas at 49th Street, which designed the area beside its bar as a dining space in 2001, stripped the starched cloths off the tables when cocktail drinkers moved in instead.

In the first three months of 2003, twenty-four of the restaurants that opened in New York—55 percent of the total—included a substantial bar or lounge area, according to the Zagat Survey, up 10 percent from the same period last year.

"Look at the most popular places, the younger, hipper restaurants, the newcomers," Mr. Zagat said. "There's an effort to provide bar space, lounge space." He cited Blue Fin in the W hotel in Times Square, and the Dos Caminos restaurants, on Park Avenue South and in SoHo, developed by Stephen R. Hanson and his company B. R. Guest. "You can barely squeeze past the bar to get to the restaurant in the back," Mr. Zagat said. "Younger people are socializing in restaurants, but they do less eating."

Danny Meyer, whose popular dining establishments include Union Square Cafe, opened in 1985, and Blue Smoke, opened last year, has increased the space given to the bar at each successive restaurant. Fifty percent of the customers at Blue Smoke's bar are there to drink, not to dine, Mr. Meyer said.

"This recession is painful," he added. "Everyone is trying to figure out how to capture customers. I'm interested in never giving up on fine dining, but I'm interested in being full all the time, too."

At Salt Bar on Clinton Street, New York's newest restaurant row, the owner and chef, Melissa O'Donnell, opened a bar that serves food, rather than a restaurant, to hedge her bets.

"People don't want five courses, but they don't want beer on the floor, either, and if they aren't interested in a meal, they stay to drink and order food anyway," she said.

At Amuse, a handsome lounge and restaurant in Chelsea that was formerly the Tonic until it was renovated and reopened two weeks ago by Gerry Hayden, its chef and an owner, a table of twenty people in their twenties and thirties sat in the bar and lounge area on Wednesday, socializing, drinking and eating side orders or desserts. No one had plans for dinner, not even next door, in Mr. Hayden's attractive dining room.

For younger New Yorkers, the advantages of an evening out over cocktails are distinct: less money, less hassle, less commitment and an ability to get home at a reasonable hour on a weeknight for those many who live outside Manhattan.

"You can get everybody you invite to come out if you just do drinks," said Holly Hunnicutt, twenty-seven, sitting with friends and colleagues from the publishing house where she works. "We order fifty baskets of French fries—that's dinner."

Ms. Hunnicutt turned back to her friends to talk. Reka Simonsen, thirty-two, who was sitting next to her in a sleeveless dress with an ink silhouette on her arm, replied, when asked, "Yes, it's a real tattoo, and yes, it's really Nancy Drew."

TITANIC

ADAPTED FROM CITARELLA

6 to 8 green grapes *(save one for garnish)*
4 or 5 ounces Cîroc vodka
Just less than 1 ounce verjus
$^1/_2$ ounce elderflower syrup
2 tablespoons Champagne sorbet, as an "iceberg" *(see Note)*
Champagne
1 raspberry

Muddle the grapes. Fill a bartender's glass two-thirds full of ice. Add the muddled grapes, vodka, verjus, and elderflower syrup. Shake until chilled. Spoon the Champagne sorbet into chilled 10-ounce martini glass and pour the shaken mixture over the sorbet. Top with Champagne and garnish with the raspberry and grape.

Yield: 1 serving

Note: To make the sorbet, place 1 cup Champagne, 1 cup elderflower syrup and 1 cup water in an ice cream maker and freeze according to instructions.

MUDWRESTLING, AND RUNNING WITH THE BULLS

MUD WRESTLER

Long Island Iced Tea

A LOT OF PEOPLE WILL TELL YOU THAT Long Island iced tea exists to waste you. Exclusively.

The drink, attributed to a bartender named Robert C. Butt at the Oak Beach Inn in Hampton Bays in the 1970s, has in it every white liquor you can think of—vodka, gin, rum and tequila. It's a frat party in a glass. College students love it. It's right up there with Jell-O shots and Sex on the Beach—a solid B plus (hey, this is an easy school), says www.student.com, a Website devoted to college life.

Martini drinkers don't drink Long Island iced tea. It hasn't got an M.B.A.

"Long Island iced tea doesn't roll off the tongue in a class environment," said Dale DeGroff, author of *The Craft of the Cocktail,* and for twelve years the head bartender at the Rainbow Room.

Long Island iced tea's biggest problem?

"It tastes great," Mr. DeGroff said.

Despite its mud-wrestler's enthusiasm for a good time, the drink is not without its finer points. Make it with fresh citrus instead of sour mix, and you have a superior Long Island iced tea, said Luis Serrano, the bartender on duty last Sunday at Bemelmans Bar at the Carlyle Hotel. Mr. Serrano, a stately but sympathetic man with sideburns and tall hair, and wearing a starched white jacket, presented his Long Island iced tea in a narrow highball glass, then topped it with a dash of Coca-Cola, poured from a small classic Coke bottle, which gives the clear drink the color of tea.

"If you shake it with the Coca-Cola, it's going to splat," he said.

At Park Avalon on Park Avenue South, a hangar-size boutique-hotel-lobby-style restaurant and bar, Jennifer Schumacher, the bartender, served her Long Island iced tea in a utilitarian-looking milkshake glass.

"What's wrong, isn't it any good?" she asked, when two minutes passed and half of it hadn't disappeared. The Park Avalon puts beer in its Long Island iced tea, too—a kind of "everybody's invited" move not inappropriate to the drink's basic thinking.

At the Duplex on Sheridan Square, the blond-goateed bartender upstairs, who gave his name as C.T., served his Long Island iced tea in a pear-shaped punch glass, shooting the Coca-Cola into it with his mixer hose like a man who could spit on your head from fourteen stories up.

"Weekends," said Mr.T., is when he gets the heavy calls for it.

Why am I not surprised?

LONG ISLAND ICED TEA

ADAPTED FROM PARK AVALON

$1/2$ ounce vodka
$1/2$ ounce gin
$1/2$ ounce white rum
$1/2$ ounce tequila
$1/2$ ounce Cointreau
$1/4$ ounce dark beer, like Bass
Splash of fresh lemon juice
Sour mix
Splash of Coke
Lemon wedge

In a shaker, mix all the liquid ingredients except sour mix and Coke; shake and pour into a 12-ounce glass with ice. Fill the glass to $1/2$ inch from the top with sour mix. Add Coke until the drink is the color of weak iced tea. Garnish with a lemon wedge.

Yield: 1 serving

READY TO ROCK

Mello Jell-O Shot

TODAY, "SHAKEN AND STIRRED" WILL TEMPORARILY BE "Stirred and Set."

Let's get jiggly with it.

Jell-O shots, one of those rare, raucous cocktails you "do," not drink, is enjoying improbable popularity this summer in New York, and it's gotten kind of fancy on itself, too. This is not the tilt, slip and slurp finger-food shot dumped from an ice cube tray and set quivering on a paper napkin on the bar, ready to rock.

Halo, a lounge on Grove Street in the West Village, serves slim wedges of Jell-O with vodka in citrus rinds. Marseille, a brasserie on Ninth Avenue at 44th Street, serves a watermelon vodka gelatin shot in a martini glass with a watermelon garnish. P.S. 1 Contemporary Art Center in Long Island City in Queens serves a cool, modernist lozenge of Jell-O and tequila—designed by William E. Massie, the New York architect who also designed the museum's urban beach installation—at its Saturday night music events.

But hey, they're Jell-O shots. Two American cultural icons in one neat kickback. Childhood to adulthood in under a second. Dessert noir.

Asia de Cuba, the sleek restaurant bar at Morgans hotel in New

York, served them when it opened in 1997, but resolve turned to jelly over their toga-party image, and Jeffrey Chodorow, the owner, pulled them off the menu.

Probably the closest you'll get to a recipe for a classic Jell-O shot (no, it's not on the box) is Ray Foley's *Ultimate Little Shooter Book II,* which calls for a cup of liquor to a packet of powdered Jell-O, a Kraft Foods product. Most of the books skip it, leaping from the Jack Rose to the julep.

Gelatin was patented in the United States in 1845 by Peter Cooper, founder of New York's Cooper Union, according to the Jell-O history pages at www.kraftfoods.com. A cough syrup manufacturer bought the patent and introduced Jell-O late in the nineteenth century.

In the twentieth century, Jell-O found its way into salads, song ("A Fine Romance" from the Rogers and Astaire musical *Swing Time* in 1936—"You take romance, I'll take Jell-O"), academic conferences (the Smithsonian Institution's 1991 symposium on Jell-O included a session on Jell-O wrestling) and outer space. Dr. Shannon W. Lucid, an American mother of three, served Jell-O to Russian astronauts on the Mir Station in 1996 on Easter Sunday.

But Jell-O, which sells or serves over a million wobbly treats in thirty-three flavors every day, wants nothing to do with the shot.

"It's a wholesome family product," said Mary Jane Kinkade, a spokesman for Kraft Foods. "We know people use it for other things. We only advocate it as a fun and delicious dessert and snack."

They never should have let it go away to school.

MELLO JELL-O SHOT

ADAPTED FROM MARSEILLE RESTAURANT

3 cups Midori melon liqueur
8 sheets baker's gelatin
2 cups watermelon juice
$^1/_2$ cup simple syrup
2 cups Stolichnaya orange vodka
$^1/_4$ cup dried currants, optional
3 ounces crème de cassis, optional

Heat 1 cup Midori with 3 sheets gelatin until dissolved. Cool. Add the remaining Midori. For each drink, pour 1$^1/_2$ ounces into a cordial glass. Leave for 20 minutes in the freezer.

Blend 1 cup watermelon juice with the simple syrup and 5 sheets gelatin. Heat until dissolved. Cool. Add the remaining watermelon juice and the vodka. Pour 1$^1/_2$ ounces to fill each glass. Dried currants soaked in crème de cassis can be added before it sets.

Yield: fifteen 3-ounce shots

A CESSPOOL OF INVENTION

Strawberry Basil Margarita

"WE HAVEN'T HAD ANY BODY SHOTS YET," said Greg Harrington, corporate beverage director for Dos Caminos, a new Mexican restaurant in New York.

A body shot is a north-of-the-border tequila drinker's technique—a shot of tequila, served with salt, on someone else's neck, and a wedge of lime, in someone else's mouth. You lick the salt off and bite into the lime, exchanging it as a kind of "Mexican kiss."

With 100 tequilas on his menu, Mr. Harrington is trying to introduce young and excitable New Yorkers to the concept of tequila as an adult's drink, like other distilled connoisseur items such as Cognac and grappa.

He has his work cut out for him.

"She fell asleep on me," a patron at Mr. Harrington's bar shouted to a drinking colleague on Wednesday night. The context was unclear.

"I like my health club," his companion roared back.

Dos Caminos, on Park Avenue South at 26th Street, is a large, loud establishment behind two tall black doors with brushed-chrome "D" and "C" door pulls that look like the world's biggest Banana Republic belt buckle.

The crowd inside could have been a reunion party for a batch of genetic clones, Class of '93. Everybody was exactly twenty-nine, to an educated guess. Most were drinking Corona beer from bottles.

Mr. Harrington's house margarita, which is Sauza Hornitos tequila with fresh strawberries and basil, is part cocktail and part cooking. An herbal, spaghetti-sauce taste underlies the fruit, making an unexpectedly handsome case for a steadily beleaguered drink.

The margarita is America's most popular cocktail. It is also, propelled by blenders and freezing machines, a cesspool of invention. Though the classic recipe calls for tequila, Cointreau and lime juice, only the once elegant daiquiri has suffered more distention from its shapely intentions.

Tequila has its own problems. People expect to see a worm sleeping at the bottom of the bottle. People expect to get kicked to the floor by drinking it.

The menu at Dos Caminos includes many new "boutique" tequilas, mellowed by aging in oak casks, like wines.

"Within the last five years, there's been a huge trend of distillers bottling tequila on their own, instead of selling it to the larger distillers," Mr. Harrington said. The liquor, distilled from the sap of the agave plant, must be produced in Mexico to be called tequila. The state of Jalisco produces 99 percent of tequila sold.

"Connoisseurs want to drink blancos," Mr. Harrington explained. "There's no 'oak' from barrel aging at all. It's 100 percent pure agave flavor. That's where climate and soil can be displayed, just like wine. A lot of people new to tequila should go to a reposado or añejo. They smooth out the acquired tastes. Drinking tequila is not something everyone is going to pick up on."

Mr. Harrington said that the standard flavors to look for in a more complex tequila are smoke, white pepper, citrus and vanilla.

Or Gucci's Rush, if you're drinking off your date.

STRAWBERRY BASIL MARGARITA

ADAPTED FROM DOS CAMINOS

2 ounces Sauza Hornitos tequila
2 ounces sliced fresh strawberries
6 torn fresh basil leaves
1 ounce fresh lime juice
Splash of simple syrup
Basil sprig

Combine all the ingredients except the basil in a shaker filled with ice. Shake and pour into a 10-ounce old-fashioned glass. Garnish with the basil sprig. Do not salt the rim.

Yield: 1 serving

PITCHER-PERFECT

Sangria

WITH THE CONFIDENCE OF PEOPLE WHO couldn't care less, the waiter, the bartender and the manager at Bottino, a fashionable restaurant and lounge in Chelsea, each denied that there was sangria on the menu last Wednesday evening. Only at a fashionable restaurant and lounge in New York do you get to see three superbly incurious minds at work together.

But a quick e-mail exchange with Danny Emerman, the owner, confirmed that there was.

Ask for it. It's good. The sangria tastes like a young, fruit-full wine—not the "hints" of strawberry or sharp citrus of wine tasting, but the things themselves.

Sangria, a Spanish drink in origin, is based on a combination of wine and liquor, fresh fruit and fruit juice. The Spanish use red Rioja and brandy.

Because Bottino's recipe calls for Recioto della Valpolicella, a sweet wine from the Veneto in Italy, Mr. Emerman characterizes his sangria loosely as "Venetian." Vernaccia di San Gimignano, the white wine that tops it off, is Tuscan. Armchair travelers can close their eyes and take their choice. It's Italian, anyway.

But sangria is built for variety, if not a woozy kind of globalization, a fact that New York restaurants seem to have discovered recently. Sangria, immensely popular, has become a citizen of the world.

Long Tan, an Asian restaurant in Park Slope in Brooklyn, serves a sangria with plum wine, which makes it Asian, said Rory Dwyer, the owner. It includes triple sec and tequila, too, which also makes the drink a version of what bartenders call a Mexican sangria. Pazo, a Midtown restaurant, serves a sangria with French fruit liqueurs. And Bolo, the celebrity chef Bobby Flay's restaurant in the Flatiron district, inspired by the cuisines of Spain, has a neo-Spanish sangria, based on white peaches, which resembles a sangria that the Spanish, in the south, call *zurra*.

Sangria's pitcher-perfect, invent-your-own quality can be entertaining. It's a lively kitchen sink of a drink. But it has the capacity to be a real swill, too—trash in any language. Ginger ale, cinnamon Red Hots, tomato juice: people have tried to flush more things down sangria than a toilet at a bar. (If you don't believe me, check out www.lisashea.com/sangria. There is now an "Atkins," "low-carb" sangria.)

Sangria means "bleeding" in Spanish. Don't run with the bulls when you make it.

SANGRIA

ADAPTED FROM BOTTINO

2 cups diced seasonal fruit, like strawberries or peaches
$^1/_2$ orange, peeled, seeded and sliced in thin wedges
Zest in thin strips of $^1/_2$ lemon
2 tablespoons sugar
1 cup Recioto della Valpolicella or port
One 750-milliliter bottle Vernaccia di San Gimignano
or other dry white wine, well chilled

Toss the diced fruit and the orange with the lemon zest, sugar and the Recioto or port and allow the fruit to macerate for about an hour.

Pour the macerated fruit and its juice into a carafe and fill with the cold white wine.

Yield: 6 servings

A GOOD MONTH FOR KITSCH

The Lover's Concerto

GOT ALOHA?

No one is denying that there isn't an enjoyable element of cocktail drinking that is—how shall I put this?—go-for-the-throat kitsch.

On Wednesday night, I jumped through the flaming hoop of flaming behavior at Trailer Park Lounge and Grill on West 23rd Street, in a triple threat: happy hour, Elvis and The Lover's Concerto, a 36-ounce frozen margarita built for two.

Kitsch is the big surf of washed-up popular culture. At Trailer Park, Tom McKay and Andy Spiro, the owners, have assembled it as scientifically as a zoo environment. And on Wednesday, at the nightly happy hour, patrons inhaled it, grazed on it, rolled in it, as if it were a natural habitat. Boxed in by Tammy Faye photos, Dolly Parton dolls, jars of Marshmallow Fluff and the side of a trailer, which forms one wall, the party animals never smelled containment.

It's been a good month for kitsch, from Martha Stewart's conviction on March 5, a kitsch legend in the making, to the governor of West Virginia's letter on March 22 to Abercrombie & Fitch, to cease and desist selling T-shirts that depict a map of the state with the phrase "It's all relative in West Virginia." Governor Bob Wise thinks it's a fun reference to Appalachian incest.

A state that can't take a joke! At Trailer Park, Governor Wise would be sold a temporary tattoo (they're available at the bar for five dollars) and directed to the poster of *Teenage Hitchhikers,* a 1974 movie. He could watch *Dragnet* on the television, where justice is served, as it should be, like beer without a glass.

And he and Ms. Stewart might share a Lover's Concerto, which is served in a volcano bowl with a shot of tequila. It would take the edge off.

At nine o'clock, Elvis came on.

"Please welcome, direct from Las Vegas . . . King Randy!" an M.C. yelped into a mike. King Randy was Elvis, *circa* the white jumpsuit. His first number was "All Shook Up." A couple next to me who appeared to be in their early twenties cowered as if Elvis were the bad Santa of a half-remembered mall experience. But a blond woman who clearly recalled the man himself was mesmerized to the point of forgetting to swallow by King Randy's pelvis impersonation.

"That's right, baby, live from '73," he told her, with a bit of aloha.

Or as Elvis tells the woman in the soaked T-shirt in *Blue Hawaii,* released in 1961, "Baby, on you, my favorite color is wet."

THE LOVER'S CONCERTO

ADAPTED FROM TRAILER PARK LOUNGE AND GRILL

6 fresh strawberries
6 limes, juiced, plus ¹/₂ lime, with pulp removed
6 ounces plus 2 ounces Sauza Hornitos tequila
2 ounces Cointreau
1 ounce Grand Marnier
2 cups frozen strawberry concentrate
4 cups lemonade, or to taste, if fresh
3 cups ice
Parasols and 2 flamingo straws

Muddle the strawberries with the lime juice. In a blender, mix all the ingredients (except the hollowed lime half and 2 ounces tequila), blending at high speed for 1 minute. Pour into a 36-ounce goblet glass. Float the lime half on top with 2 ounces of tequila poured into it. Garnish with the parasols and flamingo straws.

Yield: 1 serving for 2 people

GOOD CLEAN FUN

Minnesota Antifreeze & The Pink Puppy

MINNESOTA! LAND OF TEN THOUSAND LAKES! There is liquor in at least a few of them.

I went drinking in Uptown last week. Uptown is a "retrieved" neighborhood in the northern section of Minneapolis. It was unremarkable ten years ago; it is a strip of galleries, restaurants, boutique shopping, lifestyle chain stores and lounges and bars now.

Uptown is the West Village, the East Village, Chelsea, SoHo, TriBeCa, Lower East Side and Williamsburg, Brooklyn, of Minneapolis—if you'll allow me a moment of chauvinism, a "New York" neighborhood. (I know I'm going to get letters about that, but there you have it.)

The evening was early, but people were out. The sky was blueing down to twilight, like the deep-plush lighting in a club bathroom, clear and four dimensional and edging with a kind of liquid acid the oranges and reds and bright whites of the signs now buzzing hotly on the street. A couple walked briskly by on their way to a bar. She was wobbling on high, date-alert shoes and he was wearing his best sports dress shirt, sharply pressed and open at the collar. They were holding hands tightly as they walked. He talked on his cell phone as she wobbled forward with resolve.

To be hip and Middle American—this is not something New Yorkers think much about, unless they're from Minnesota and they've recently moved to New York.

At the bar at Chino Latino, which looked about a city block long and was backlighted with yellow LED-like light, a young crowd in baseball caps and beautifully conditioned hair hoisted beer bottles and cocktail glasses and jammed themselves together happily like a child balling a piece of white bread.

And at the bar at Tonic of Uptown, a new lounge and restaurant that opened in March, Minneapolis seemed just fine. Ciao, Manhattan. Or just, "Later."

The cocktail nation is no longer a turn of phrase for a trend or phenomenon. It is a demographic, with a vote. Cocktails are now an established entertainment, like going to the movies. And new American grills, or lounges, like Tonic owe more to multiplexes than traditional bars.

Tonic is a three-story industrial space with steel catwalks, a stone bar lighted blue beneath it, flat-screen televisions and blue tufted clamshell banquettes against one wall for diners—a lounge made from parts, several nightlife trends of the last several years, soldered together.

The clientele doesn't notice the seams. After-work groups, single blond women in pairs, graying bachelors who still want to be players, young men in design-distressed jeans jackets and Abercrombie & Fitch neck chokers—the clientele is a bit of a grab bag, too, as seems to befit Uptown. You've got one obvious place to go. You go to it. (The upstart downmarket neighborhood in Minneapolis as of this writing is Northeast, where you drink at the Sample Room or Kye's Polonais Room, which is a perennial and features "the world's most dangerous polka band." I'm not going to argue with that.)

At Tonic, the generation named Britney walked up and down the steel staircases, balancing their martini glasses with perfect form, gripping them gingerly at the rim.

I ordered a Pink Puppy from the specialty cocktail list, which was labeled "Elixirs: So Many Choices, So Little Time." Who's in a hurry in Minneapolis? Only your hormones, if you're single.

"All *right,*" my junior varsity bartender, Graham, said in response to my choice.

The Pink Puppy is a lemon vodka, Campari and grapefruit drink with a salt rim. The salt helps a basic beach cabana cocktail. It's translucent and pastel, but it has the sting of a jellyfish.

Also on the menu is the Minnesota Antifreeze.

"Mixing it up!" Graham said, when I ordered that next.

The Minnesota Antifreeze is green and thick, like its namesake. You would not want to drink it until you are trapped in your car in a snowstorm, and looking for a way to make yourself happy to die in the cold. You might want to try the antifreeze in the car first. The Minnesota Antifreeze is disgusting, and I think brain health would be an issue, if you finished one. It looks and acts more like glue-sniffing than a cocktail.

Good clean fun it's not, and that will always make me scratch my head about places like Minnesota, where what becomes dangerous on the coasts could in reality be imports from the heartland, as waves of young professionals continue to emigrate to Los Angeles and New York, bringing their cocktail habits with them.

I'd call it an innocent versa vice, if you will.

MINNESOTA ANTIFREEZE

ADAPTED FROM TONIC OF UPTOWN

1 1/2 ounces Shakers
1/2 ounce blue curaçao
1/2 ounce Midori melon liqueur
1 ounce pineapple juice
Rock candy

Shake all the ingredients together with ice; strain into a chilled martini glass. Garnish with rock candy.

Yield: 1 serving

THE PINK PUPPY

ADAPTED FROM TONIC OF UPTOWN

Salt
1 1/4 ounces Absolut Citron
1/4 ounce Campari
Grapefruit juice
Lime wedge

Fill a 14-ounce glass (rimmed with salt) with ice. Add the vodka and juice. Float Campari on top. Garnish with a lime wedge.

Yield: 1 serving

FEMMES FATALES

LUCY LIU

Shanghai Cosmo

IF NEW YORKERS HAD TO NAME THEIR POISON, it might be overexposure. No, it's not a cocktail, though it would be a stiff one if it were. It's a strange sort of death wish, to go out as often as possible, to be on the scene and to be seen, and yet not to be too many places too many times. You don't want to get old, as they say.

Of course, New York's got a brilliant solution that keeps people here like a drug. It comes up with new places before you get old in the old ones.

The cosmopolitan was a kind of fast debutante that showed up in the 1980s and 1990s—the Cornelia Guest of cocktails. Many people claimed it, like dates who had been dumped at a club. (Ocean Spray, the cranberry juice bottler, already had on the books a very similar drink, the "Harpoon." What's in a name?—celebrity, or nothing.)

The cosmopolitan, which took on a life of its own, hit all the right spots, networked with the wonder women of the era, like Madonna and the characters in *Sex and the City*—part empowerment, part buzz-on. It was not for men. It was a way of going out without them, in fact. Nicole Beland, the author of *The Cocktail Jungle: A Girl's Field Guide to Shaking and Stirring,* calls it a "girlie martini."

After the first few trips around the block, the cosmopolitan dropped the basics, which included cranberry juice, and started hitting the wardrobe racks. Outfits became crucial: the ginger cosmo, the plum cosmo. By 2000, there were as many cosmopolitans as Sykes or Hilton sisters.

When 66, the new Jean-Georges Vongerichten restaurant at 66 Leonard Street in TriBeCa, opened several weeks ago, it had to have a cosmopolitan, said Chuck Simeone, the beverage director for Jean-Georges Management. It is still a top-selling drink and an important style item for a specialty cocktail menu, he said.

The Shanghai Cosmo at 66, which was created in character with the restaurant's Chinese theme, is a Lucy Liu of a drink—it lowers its eyes and kicks, the Asian Charlie's Angel.

"It's a powerful drink, but it's designed so it doesn't have a liquor taste," said Mr. Simeone, its creator. "You have a couple and it's . . . there." In addition to vodka there is sake, and four fruit juices, from sweet to tart.

Served in the low light of 66's minimal-chic lounge (you feel as if your head is on a dimmer), the work of the architect Richard Meier, the Shanghai Cosmo, pale red and suspiciously smooth, contributes to the impression of being presented with an opiate, not alcohol, in a den, not a bar. On Tuesday night, the waitress had a shoulder tattoo. Yes, it was a dragon, but maybe it was Jean-Georges issue, like the Vivienne Tam uniforms.

The cocktail played one of the oldest of games. It hesitated for the first few sips, content to be pretty, and then the trick went up my sleeve.

SHANGHAI COSMO

ADAPTED FROM 66

1 1/2 ounces Skyy vodka
1 ounce plum sake
1 ounce cranberry juice
Splash of guanabana juice
Splash of pineapple juice
Splash of lime juice
French-cut lemon twist

Shake the liquid ingredients with ice in a shaker. Strain into a martini glass. Garnish with the lemon twist.

Yield: 1 serving

THAT OLE BLACK MAGIC

Campari d'Asti & Raspberry Gin Fizz

I DRINK FOR A LIVING, which technically makes me a heavy-weight drinker. But there are times when you know you have to take the crown off and pass it down the bar.

Last night was one of those times. I stopped into BLT Steak, or Bistro Laurent Tourondel, a new restaurant on East 57th Street, to check out Fred Dexheimer's specialty cocktail list. Mr. Dexheimer is the beverage director and sommelier.

"Cocktails are my children," he said in a telephone conversation. Mr. Dexheimer has also worked at Cello, 66 and Gramercy Tavern, creating drinks.

BLT Steak is a formulaically suave French-modern New York bistro in design—the basic boil-down from Jean Michel Frank to the contemporary schools of Christian Liaigre and Christophe Delcourt.

I ordered the Campari d'Asti, a bright copper-colored drink, which is a Campari and soda with ultra-soda: Moscato d'Asti. It's a logical idea, and it's good. I also tried the Raspberry Gin Fizz, which has fresh raspberries muddled into it and a wallop of fresh mint. Also good.

Mr. Dexheimer's fizz's uniqueness, though, is its color—not a light raspberry soda-pop red, but a deep, mature, Baroque painter's red. Like blood, or velvet. That's when the experts stepped in.

Two society ladies, the "ladies who lunch," sat next to me at the bar, dressed in expensive day clothes—dark suits, light blouses and gold—that translated easily to evening. They were as thin as the stems of the white wineglasses that sat in front of them on the bar. They picked from a dish of olives and a dish of almonds. Have you ever watched someone make an olive a three-course meal? I have.

"What a beautiful color," said the lady sitting farthest from me, society at work. "What is that you're drinking?"

We talked. We talked about cocktails. We talked about drinking. The lady next to me was from New Orleans, which from her description, and fairly historical hearsay, is a good place to drink. I mentioned this, to be polite. I got the first of several well-manicured, light taps on the sleeve as camaraderie developed, and a surprised look. Genuine surprise, on the spur of the moment, is something that society ladies are extremely good at—without equal in fact.

"You have to know how to drink to *live* there," she said. "We drink round the clock: twenty-four hours, seven days a week."

She added, "There's no such thing as Sunday there," referring to the blue laws in other states, including New York. Then she remembered the drive-in daiquiri bars, and threw those into the discussion.

Well, here, take this and put it on your head.

My new friend gave me the names of establishments where the drinking was best. They included Eleven 79 on Annunciation Street, owned by a gentleman named Joe Segreto, who is also a sometime filmmaker.

"He did a documentary film on . . . who was Keely Smith's husband?" my friend asked. The question was like the birthdate on her driver's license. "You're making me think. I don't like to think."

Dorothy Jacqueline Keely Smith is a big-band singer who was popular in the 1950s and married to Louie Prima, a band leader. They had a hit in 1958 with "That Ole Black Magic."

I asked about Bourbon Street.

"I'm one of those uptown ladies," she said. "I avoid Bourbon Street." My friend, instead, detailed the Mad Hatters' Luncheon, an annual event sponsored by the Women's Guild for the benefit of the New Orleans Opera Association.

"Drinks? Are you kidding?" she asked, when I asked if alcohol was served. "They start drinking at ten-thirty. Mimosas . . . Champagne. Skip the mimosa part."

We reflected on this together, the three of us. I admit that the greater part of my reflection was just being stunned. It was like finding out that what you consider your professional role is what others would consider an audition.

My new friend was kind. She invited me to New Orleans, and gave me two tips when there: get invited to a party, and drink water between drinks.

"There are some straight people there, who work," she said, in an effort, ever the society lady, to make me feel welcome. "A few..."

CAMPARI D'ASTI

ADAPTED FROM BLT STEAK

$^1/_2$ ounce Campari
$^1/_2$ ounce Cointreau or triple sec
1 ounce fresh grapefruit juice
$^3/_4$ ounce Moscato d'Asti
Grapefruit wedge

Pour the ingredients over ice into a mixing glass, shake and serve over crushed ice in a wineglass. (If crushed ice is not available, pour the mixed product with the shaker's ice into the glass.) Top with the Moscato d'Asti. Garnish with the wedge of grapefruit.

Yield: 1 serving

RASPBERRY GIN FIZZ

ADAPTED FROM BLT STEAK

5 fresh or frozen raspberries
5 fresh mint sprigs
1 teaspoon sugar
1½ ounces Boodles British Gin
½ ounce Cointreau
¼ ounce fresh lime juice
1 ounce soda water
Fresh mint sprig

Muddle the raspberries, mint and sugar in a mixing glass until the mint is broken into small pieces and the raspberries are crushed. Pour the gin, Cointreau and lime juice into a mixer, add ice and shake. After shaking, pour the soda into the mixing glass to integrate it with the raspberry mixture. Pour into a highball glass and garnish with a sprig of mint.

Yield: 1 serving

UNCONVENTIONAL BEAUTY

Martini Rossi Rosso

WHILE ULTRA-PREMIUM GINS AND VODKAS make splashy entrances in martinis all over town, segregating drinkers into two camps like a turf war at a club, no one is paying much attention to what's going in on their arms.

It's vermouth, of course, and generally it is not encouraged to speak up.

The dry martini, with a minimum of dry vermouth, is the little black dress of drinks, and that's what the young martini moguls want a hot handhold on. You order it dirty if you're freaky.

But some of the more stylish players on the cocktail scene are hitting on a different flavor: sweet vermouth.

Sweet vermouth is, like dry vermouth, a brandy-fortified wine mixed with botanicals like herbs, flowers and roots. Sweet vermouth is closer in taste to what people associate with a standard aperitif base, like Lillet or Dubonnet.

Sweet vermouth is a component in two popular aperitivo-like cocktails, the Negroni and the Americano, each of which includes Campari. And the Manhattan, one of the nineteenth-century drinks that began to reduce the fanciful art of the cocktail to a science by the twentieth century, prefers sweet vermouth, though it can include dry, too. BLT Steak, a new bistro on East 57th Street, is serving a bourbon Manhattan, with a reserve bourbon, as a house specialty. Sweet vermouth handles it like a pro, letting it brag and softening the bluster.

At La Bottega, in the Maritime Hotel, on Ninth Avenue between Sixteenth and Seventeenth Streets, the bar serves a Martini Rossi Rosso, which is a vodka martini with sweet rather than dry vermouth.

The switch is a clever one. Though the taste is new, the idea is old. Among the major branches of the martini's genealogical tree is the Martinez, a gin and sweet vermouth cocktail, mixed in a reverse proportion to the modern martini, that presses a paternity claim called into question by the fact that no one can agree on who fathered the original Martinez, or where or with what.

With its varnished wood ceiling, La Bottega, scarred and mirrored and yellow-lighted, is like drinking inside an antiquated jukebox, one in Havana that no one has the money to replace.

(Last Sunday, three drunken men with three sober women were at the bar celebrating the University of Connecticut's supremacy on the basketball courts—what a sports watcher called "Coed Huskie Mania." Both the men's and women's teams went on to win National Collegiate Athletic Association championship titles on Monday and Tuesday nights.)

My Martini Rossi Rosso was tinted ruby, a novel touch, and not sweet as you might expect. It is a martini with a mind of its own. Slightly bitter, with traces of orange blossom and spice, the cocktail has what film and fashion agents call "unconventional beauty."

You decide if you can be comfortable with that.

MARTINI ROSSI ROSSO

ADAPTED FROM LA BOTTEGA
AT THE MARITIME HOTEL

$4^1/_2$ ounces vodka
$1^1/_2$ ounces sweet vermouth
$^1/_8$ ounce orange bitters
Orange twist

In a shaker filled with ice, shake the vodka and sweet vermouth. Strain into a chilled martini glass. Add a healthy dash of orange bitters. Garnish with orange twist.

Yield: 1 serving

SWEET BOOZE OF YOUTH

Yellow Desert Rose

PIONEER, BY ITS OWN DESCRIPTION, is a Western saloon on what could be called the upper stretch of the Wild Wild East Side—that strip of still-singles or singles-again bars and restaurants on Third Avenue above 72nd Street.

The establishment is pale yellow, and last Wednesday the women, wearing sweaters as scarves, drank beer from bottles, but . . . politely. The smooth-faced men wore tattersall shirts and khaki or linen shorts. There were buck deer heads mounted on the walls, and a ballgame was on the television at the bar.

Pioneer has done a peculiar thing, which is to put a Southern Comfort cocktail, the Yellow Desert Rose, on its menu. Southern Comfort is not something I had thought about since it crossed my lips thirty-six years ago, at age fifteen. It made fine drinking in high school, and then, after one night of too much, it was gone—the sweet booze of youth.

The company that owns the brand, Brown-Forman in Louisville, Kentucky, admits as much. Southern Comfort is most popular with drinkers twenty-one to twenty-nine years old. Brown-Forman, which also markets Jack Daniel's, calls it a "rite of passage" brand. (After a drop-off in midlife, the curve comes back up with drinkers over forty-nine—the fumes of nostalgia, maybe.)

"People discover it early in their drinking," said Dana Allen, the global creative director of Southern Comfort. "It's sweeter and easier to drink." That would be me, stuffing a package of gum in my mouth before going home after a basement party in 1967.

Southern Comfort, which is technically a liqueur because it is a blend of whiskey and fruit flavors (including peach), was developed in 1874 by M. W. Heron at his bar in New Orleans.

Today, it is in the midst of what Brown-Forman calls a revitalization that involves a new bottle and a television and Website campaign "Between Friends," which features a fictional cast of young professionals negotiating adulthood with good times and Southern Comfort. (The brand's strongest markets right now are California in the United States, Canada, and Britain.)

"It's about not being pretentious," said Paul Tuell, the brand manager, who called that quality "different from a martini moment."

The crux is to retool Southern Comfort's reputation as a honky-tonk drink without losing its rasp.

Southern Comfort's patron saint, of course, is Janis Joplin, the Texan boa-bedecked, crash-and-burn blues-rock goddess of the late 1960s—a truth so enormous that Brown-Forman is afraid to deny it.

"The reason the brand grew so incredibly was Janis Joplin," Ms. Allen said.

Ms. Joplin would have made an unlikely figure at the bar at Pioneer, though she might have gotten patrons through a chorus of "Oh, Lord, won't you buy me a Mercedes-Benz?"

But the Yellow Desert Rose, which includes tequila and orange juice, too, stood her in good stead—one part heart, one part gut. The kind of cocktail that makes you think you can sing, and lets you go where your voice takes you.

YELLOW DESERT ROSE

ADAPTED FROM PIONEER

1 ounce Southern Comfort
1 ounce tequila
Orange juice
Grenadine
Pineapple, orange and lime slices

Shake the liquors with ice; strain and pour into a 5-ounce Collins glass over fresh ice. Fill the glass with orange juice. Top off with a drop of grenadine and garnish with pineapple, orange and lime slices.

Yield: 1 serving

A TOUCH OF EVIL

La Paloma

"COME ON, READ MY FUTURE TO ME," says Hank Quinlan, a corrupt Texas cop, to Tanya, a Mexican border town madame, in Orson Welles's *Touch of Evil*. Welles plays Quinlan, and Marlene Dietrich is Tanya.

"You haven't got any," she replies.

I was sitting at the bar at Sueños, a new Mexican restaurant at 311 West 17th Street, thinking about this recently.

Time for a drink.

At the bar, Sueños ("dreams" in Spanish) has the fever-dream quality of Welles's 1958 film: shot at night with garish light, too dark and too bright at the same time. You go down a few steps, through a service corridor, and arrive—the kind of space high-stakes dog-fights take place in. The hostess wore a black leather gaucho hat last Wednesday. The bartender and waiters were dressed in drab khaki shirts and trousers, like the Mexican police. You get the impression that if you woke up the next morning and went back to look for the bar, it wouldn't be there. There would be that dryness in your throat, and the name: "La Paloma."

I ordered La Paloma. The cocktail is as basic as a bet: liquor and soda, tequila and Mexican Squirt, which is a grapefruit soda. Squirt is a sweeter, tarter version of citrus sodas like Fresca. (Jarritos is another popular brand, and flavors include mandarin orange and tamarind.) On the evenings when, I suspect, the staff drinks all the Squirt, Sueños substitutes a blend of grapefruit juice, Grand Marnier and 7Up—a margarita with a couple of extra mariachis.

Working with Steve Olson, a beverage consultant, Sue Torres, the owner and chef of Sueños, based La Paloma on a cocktail she was served in Mexico at the Don Julio ranch, owned by the tequila family, where they grow their agave.

"They said, 'We're going to make you a real margarita, a Mexican margarita,'" Ms. Torres recalled. It was Squirt, tequila and lime.

Ms. Torres is half Italian and half Puerto Rican, she explained.

"I was exposed to Latin food until I was ten or twelve," she said. "Great-grandmothers in Corona, massive meals—my dad would make *arroz*. I always loved that food."

La Paloma, which translates as "the dove," and also, similarly, as a meek or a mild person, is an aptly named cocktail. It acts like it's never held a gun before, and then it blows the tin can into the air. Perversely, it tastes better with grapefruit soda than grapefruit juice.

Sueños also serves a Cosmolito—a Mexican cosmopolitan. It brought back to mind the black-haired Marlene Dietrich as Tanya in *Touch of Evil* and a framed letter hanging in Ms. Dietrich's apartment on Park Avenue, which I had the opportunity to view when Sotheby's helped her son, Michael Riva, sell its contents.

Dietrich reacted with fire to Welles's idea that she play the madame in a Mexican brothel, and demanded an explanation for the offer.

"Haven't you ever heard of type-casting?" he wrote back.

LA PALOMA

ADAPTED FROM SUEÑOS

1½ ounces Herradura Hacienda del Cristero Blanco tequila
¾ ounce fresh lime juice (from half a lime), plus 1 lime slice
4 ounces Mexican Squirt soda, or
1 ounce fresh grapefruit juice and 3 ounces 7-Up

Pour the tequila over ice in a tall highball or Collins glass. Add the lime juice. Add Squirt or a substitute. Stir and garnish with a slice of lime.

Yield: 1 serving

OH MY GOODNESS, I'M FEELING IT

Me and Mrs. Jones

I WENT UPTOWN LAST WEEK LOOKING FOR MY own version of house—drinks, that is.

On Wednesday night, Harlem was not hot.

It was twenty-one degrees outside, and midweek—the dead of everything. At Ekow, a new white-on-white unmarked lounge on Frederick Douglass Boulevard at 113th Street, the doorman, stunned by boredom or the cold, forgot to make me wait outside. There was basketball on the projection television, and a sparse neighborhood crowd hugged the bar and corners, drinking. The martini glasses were huge and the house drinks were sweet.

The Ekow Plus has two kinds of fruit schnapps in it, like twin Playmates: apple and peach. The staff, wearing tight white jersey outfits, was sweet, too, but it was artificial sweetener.

"I've never heard of it," my waitress said with a smile when asked how to get to Jimmy's Uptown, the most conspicuous of the Harlem re-Renaissance night spots. The bartender talked over us on her cell phone. It was too cold, and too Wednesday, for that.

At Jimmy's Uptown, the modernist moon-palace dining room was empty, there were no house drinks, and it was the bartender's first night. I asked.

"I don't know how to make that," she replied to a request for a martini. The busboy explained it to her. She overdosed a Thug Passion, which is a cognac drink popular uptown, with Alizé. (The cocktail, immortalized in a rap, "Thug Passion," by Tupac Shakur in 1996, is the drink "guaranteed to get the pussy wet and the dick hard.")

She produced a shot of whiskey without help. Beginner's luck.

At Moca, a lounge on Frederick Douglass Boulevard at 119th Street, the house drinks were perfect. I wish several didn't exist, including the French Kiss martini, which was its own best reason for never opening your mouth.

Native, on Lenox Avenue at 118th Street, is a small corner restaurant. The house is home-style—on Wednesday, it was comfortably crowded at the bar with people who knew each other well.

Brian Washington-Palmer, the owner, recently developed a specialty cocktail list, which was news to Boi Jackson, the bartender—that night's news.

"Make me a stew? Give me a goat!" said Ms. Jackson, wearing black-on-black, when I ordered the Me and Mrs. Jones, one of the inventions Mr. Washington-Palmer shared with me by e-mail message that day. "Me and Mrs. Jones," recorded by Billy Paul, was a Billboard No. 1 hit in 1972. (As was "I Am Woman," by Helen Reddy, and "American Pie," by Don McLean.)

Using my printout, Ms. Jackson mixed Champagne, Chambord, dry vermouth and lime with a bartender's instinct.

I shared the glass with the woman sitting next to me, who was drinking a mojito.

"Oh, this is good," she said. "Can I have one?" She passed it on. "Oh, my goodness, I'm feeling it," the next person said.

Ms. Jackson took three orders quickly.

We and Mrs. Jones; we got a thing going on.

ME AND MRS. JONES

ADAPTED FROM NATIVE

$^1/_2$ ounce dry vermouth
$^1/_2$ ounce fresh or Rose's Lime Juice
1 ounce Chambord
5 ounces Champagne of choice
1 or 2 dashes of maraschino cherry juice
Dash of bitters
Maraschino cherry

Chill a 7-ounce Champagne glass. Rinse the glass with the vermouth (reserve the vermouth). Add the lime juice and Chambord. Fill the glass with Champagne. Top with the reserved vermouth, cherry juice and bitters. Garnish with a cherry.

Yield: 1 serving

A TOUGH SELL

The Dirty Jane

NEW YORK IS A DIRTY TOWN. And not much is dirtier, or more New York, than the house drink at Jane, a restaurant in the West Village—the Dirty Jane. It's a pickled martini. Any questions?

The Dirty Jane is a gimmick, and it is also a great cocktail. (I've put my resignation in a sealed envelope; to be opened upon this recommendation.) Part martini, part deli sandwich, it is a vodka martini, no vermouth, with a wedge of pickled green tomato instead of an olive. A splash of the pickle brine makes it "dirty," as a splash of olive brine would make it a straight "dirty martini." The drink itself is a clear liquid.

"It took me forever to try it," said Autumn Kohl, the bartender who recently served me the Dirty Jane. She knows a tough sell when she sees it. The raspberry mojitos and passion fruit cosmopolitans do a lot better on your average night.

With Ms. Kohl's encouragement, I toothpicked and ate the garnish. Even the green tomato was good—slightly garlicky and now pickled with vodka, too. Jane, an American bistro with a modern design, sets out toasted pumpkin seeds at its concrete bar. The Dirty Jane, which is salty, is that rare cocktail that works well with food.

The bad news, not so bad: to lock lips with this drink (and I swear, that night, it was love) you have to make it at home, unless you walk into Jane. You will not have much luck asking for green tomato pickles at most bars. You might not want to try just yet, if you're a regular anywhere.

The inventor of the Dirty Jane, Glenn Harris, Jane's executive chef and an owner, is a Brighton Beach boy.

"I kind of grew up with it," said Mr. Harris, thirty-two. "When we were kids, sixteen years old, there was a large Russian immigration, and I had a lot of Russian friends. We would go down to the boardwalk, to the food stands.

"They never ID'ed anyone. You eat all this greasy food—cutlets and potatoes. We would do vodka shots, and chase it with pickle juice from the barrels. When we first opened Jane, we called it [the drink] a Little Odessa, but it didn't sell."

Mr. Harris said he thought it was only a question of positioning to get the Dirty Jane to the right customer.

"It's a low-fat play on a dirty martini; this is cleaner," he said.

"There's a dirty-martini drinker out there," he added, characterizing that drinker as "smoky." Mr. Harris himself was husky on the telephone.

"I'm a little under the weather today," he said, then he brightened. "Maybe I need to go down to the boardwalk."

How does a Borscht Mary sound?

THE DIRTY JANE

ADAPTED FROM JANE

2 ounces Ketel One vodka
1 ounce liquid from pickled green tomatoes
Pickled green tomato wedge

In a shaker filled with ice, combine the vodka and pickling liquid. Shake and strain into a chilled martini glass. Garnish the rim with a tomato wedge.

Yield: 1 serving

THE ORIGINAL UNCOSMOPOLITAN

Adam and Eve

I DRINK IN THE AFTERNOON. OCCASIONALLY.

Amuse, a restaurant on West 18th Street, has a very pleasant cocktail called the Adam and Eve, which is kind of the drink equivalent of meeting a friend for lunch on your day off. It's engaging and easy and a little intellectual—nothing too tough—and you feel like you're meeting it for the first time and like you've known it all your life. Just like a friend you enjoy seeing, and perhaps don't see often enough. Let's do lunch.

Amuse is the old Harvey's, which was a tavern-style bar and restaurant of long standing. The varnished paneling and scarred bar are still there, though Amuse has an iPod-like overlay of mod furnishing: cream-colored banquettes and brushed-steel wall sconces and there are ingot-shaped cream cloth lamps hanging over the bar. The tin ceiling is painted ivory white and the hexagonal ceramic floor tiles—Irish-bar men's-room-chic—have stayed in place.

Atypically, the lounge's decor is attractive by day. It doesn't suffer that nightclub hangover look which many lounges do at noon, as though the sun was an out-of-towner's mistake.

Miles Davis, the jazz trumpeter who seems to have a lock on cool-tone background music, played in the background one afternoon recently as I ordered an Adam and Eve.

The Adam and Eve is an apple martini, in genre. Or an apple side-car—it is Calvados based. Or an apple cosmopolitan. It has white cranberry juice, too. But it is a very very elegant drink. As elegant as the idea of taking time off, on the spur of the moment, because you decide you deserve it. Wake up and make lunch plans. Call the office. Why not.

The cocktail is pale gold. The apple in the Garden of Eden was a Golden Delicious, apparently. And the drink is a temptation. As for Adam's Eve, the original uncosmopolitan, who had never seen an apple before, let alone an apple martini, we can only be grateful she didn't stumble upon a bartender serving these.

I can live with being kicked out of the yard. But you never live down being kicked out of a bar. Especially in broad daylight.

ADAM AND EVE

ADAPTED FROM AMUSE

2 ounces Camut 12-year-old Calvados
1 ounce Cointreau
1 ounce white cranberry juice
Splash ($1/2$ ounce) of Mathilde Poire liqueur
Sparkling French cider
Lady apple or a slice of regular green apple

Shake all the ingredients, except the cider and lady apple, with ice. Strain into a chilled martini glass, add a splash of French cider, and garnish with lady apple or apple slice.

Yield: 1 serving

DARK AS A MOTIVE

Bella Donna

"TITANIC SINKS NIGHTLY!" Bally's big bright sign S O S-es on the Strip. It gives new meaning to last call.

Drinking seems kind of redundant in Las Vegas. You could just walk around, and save your money. But I hit a few bars last Thursday, looking for a cocktail. And that's when I met the Bella Donna.

It was at Nectar, the *Wallpaper*-generation lounge-style bar at the Bellagio. Las Vegas has discovered young people recently, and the biospheric casino hotels on the boulevard now include places to drink reminiscent of airport VIP rooms, whose design the twenty-five-to-thirty-four demographic considers a peak of Western culture, not unlike temples to the Greeks.

At the MGM Grand, it is Zuri, a new velvet and blue halogen bar, which offers infused vodkas and the Gen Y martinis that read like waiters reciting the ingredients in dining specials. At Treasure Island at the Mirage, it is Mist, a liquid-crystal red lounge which opened last week. What the honeymooning cowboys and the housewives on holiday, lighted like fiends by slot machine screens and drinking from double-pint paper cups, think of all this is unclear.

Randy Morelock, the bartender on duty at Nectar, wore a graphite-gray silk satin shirt with a black necktie and looked exactly like George Hamilton, *circa* 1975 (Jacqueline Susann's *Once Is Not Enough*—you have my word).

Mr. Morelock served me my first drink, a Bungee Jumper, from a house cocktail menu that was divided thematically into "Mild," "Wild" and "Feeling Fuzzy." The Bungee Jumper, a lemon drink with citron vodka and limoncello, was "Wild," but it was also a bit of a picnic. The Impromptu Martini, cocktail No. 2, from the "Feeling Fuzzy" section, was a knuckle-whitening swerve from common sense, involving sherry instead of vermouth and a caperberry. You would have to drink one quickly to enjoy the next one.

With two sipped but unswilled cocktails between us on the brushed-steel bar, Mr. Morelock, who worked in Bellagio's casino before being moved to Nectar by Marie Maher, the general manager with whom he develops drinks, decided to tip his hand.

"Let me send you something on the house," he said, as though the house had gone dim and a fresh deck sat centered and spotlighted before me.

It was as dark as a motive, and smoky on the tongue, like a kiss between cigarettes. It didn't even have a name. There was sugar on the rim, but wait, there was an adult spice in the sugar, too—a coarse powder of freshly ground cinnamon. I felt as if the drink was watching me, sleepy-eyed, to see the effects begin.

Mr. Morelock and Ms. Maher have christened the new cocktail the Bella Donna. It will be introduced at Nectar this week on their winter/spring menu. The drink is to be featured as a "Wild" item, but there's nothing in Las Vegas that isn't crazy like a fox.

I'd put money on it's being a winner.

BELLA DONNA

ADAPTED FROM NECTAR

Sugar mix *(combine 1 tablespoon each of sugar and ground cinnamon)*
1 ounce Gosling's Black Seal Rum
1 ounce Amaretto di Saronno
2 tablespoons fresh sour mix *(combine 1 tablespoon each*
of sugar, water, lemon and lime juices)

Rim the martini glass with the sugar mix. Shake the rum, amaretto and sour mix with ice. Strain into a glass and serve.

Yield: 1 serving

DRINK ANOTHER DAY

The Vesper

HERE'S A COCKTAIL WITH MORE ALIASES than a spy with a franchise.

The Vesper is apparently, depending on whom you believe, either the original James Bond martini or an original drink unrelated to the Bond martini that was created by either Bond and his creator, Ian Fleming, or by Fleming's friend Ivor Bryce, a Texas oil millionaire, with Fleming, or by Gilberto Preti, a London bartender, in honor of Fleming's first Bond book, *Casino Royale*.

The cocktail appears in the book and is named for Vesper Lynd, the double agent who is Bond's lady interest until her suicide over split allegiances to the free world and the evil empire of the Soviet Union. Bond dedicates the drink to the "violet hour," a beautiful evocation of the ethos of the cocktail. Nice, Sir James.

The Vesper itself is a double agent, and the Cold War in a glass—both gin and vodka, in deference to Britain and Russia, and Lillet, with a twist of lemon. Every liaison requires lingerie and something tart, right?

But the Lillet is what keeps the cocktail's gin-to-vodka fusion in check, or it's just another drink fatale. Bond was originally a gin drinker, appropriately for an English agent, and the Vesper was a gin drink. The now familiar Bond martini, with its strict instruction to be shaken, not stirred, and its large vodka measure, is the love child of an early deal with Smirnoff vodka when the Bond movies became popular. (Humphrey Bogart drinks Gordon's gin in *The African Queen,* in 1951, one of the grandfathers of endorsement deals.)

Despite Bond's famed finickiness about what and how he drinks, he hasn't been true to himself, at least in the movies. He drinks mint juleps in *Goldfinger* and rum Collinses in *Thunderball.* And in spite of his expensive defection from Smirnoff to Finlandia vodka this year in *Die Another Day,* he seems to favor mojitos.

Only Felix Leiter, the CIA agent who is Bond's best friend in the series until he gets taken out of service by a shark in *Live and Let Die,* remains faithful to drinking the Bond martini. But then, that's what best friends are for—they, at least, remember why everyone's supposed to like you.

At Pravda, at 281 Lafayette Street in New York, Jason Kosmas, the bar manager, makes his Vesper as if it were being served behind the Iron Curtain, with three parts vodka to one part gin, a reverse of the original recipe. Pravda is a vodka bar, and Mr. Kosmas thinks vodka is what people want at the moment.

The Vesper has a reputation for being an aphrodisiac, but what wouldn't with a short list of strong liquors in it?

With its adroit international accent, it has, like an emblem of espionage itself, a way of making you talk.

Engage it. But beware. And live to drink another day.

THE VESPER

ADAPTED FROM PRAVDA

3 ounces Stolichnaya Gold vodka
1 ounce Beefeater dry gin
$^1/_4$ ounce white Lillet
Lemon twist

Pour the ingredients into a Boston shaker. Fill with ice and shake vigorously. Strain into a chilled martini glass. Garnish with a twist.

Yield: 1 serving

MEN JUST THROW DVD PLAYERS OUT

The Vamp

SCOTCH HAS A PROBLEM WITH WOMEN. Men account for 80 percent of those who drink Scotch whiskey in the United States. Last year, Dewar's, the only Scotch that sells over a million cases annually in the United States, enlisted Playboy Enterprises in a major marketing campaign—a series of Vegas-style lounge parties with bunnies and club keys that recalled the days when "Scotch was king," Dewar's explained.

But when is a Rat Pack just a bunch of rats?

"It's about sophistication, not being a Neanderthal," said Charles Ho, marketing manager for Dewar's, after a hard laugh, man to man, at the question.

Think of the Vamp as a bit of sensitivity training. Dewar's asked Julie Reiner, an owner of the Flatiron Lounge on West 19th Street, to invent a Scotch cocktail. The classic, the rob roy, which is Scotch and vermouth, hadn't had a date in a while, and Dewar's, which sponsors tastings for graduate students—its twenty-to-thirty-something demographic target—started seeing women show up last year, to the tune of 50 percent. Bartenders were telling the company that women were bored with the cosmopolitan and other women's drinks. Dewar's, a "brown liquor" staple whose reign took a hit in the 1980s when vodka ascended, got thirsty for sales.

"There are close to four million new adults entering the market every year, and that includes women," said Frank Walters, director of research at M. Shanken Communications, a beverage research company in New York, speaking of what he called a baby boomlet that will continue until 2012.

And that means drinkers.

On Wednesday evening, the Flatiron Lounge, which has an Art Deco theme, looked like a speakeasy open to the sidewalk. The Vamp isn't on the menu yet; you have to ask for it—a kind of "Sam's sister sent me" knock on the door.

The drink is Scotch and fresh orange juice, smoky but citrusy, too, like having a cigarette with breakfast. Because it's bunnies and not rats getting the pitch now, Dewar's is promoting Scotch as carbohydrate free, and the Vamp as lower in sugar than the sweeter women's drinks. But because it's people braced on bar stools and not weight machines, that's nice but not the point.

The Vamp is not helped by its publicists, who issued the following statement: "Julie has created a new drink for the modern woman who can keep up with the boys. The woman who manages her own finances, uses power tools, fixes the DVD player and runs business meetings while wearing very high heels." Men just throw DVD players out.

Ms. Reiner, a friendly woman who has the experienced patience of a bartender, said that the politics of cocktails and "how women don't really drink Scotch" annoyed her. "It's not that women don't drink Scotch," she explained.

"Women come in and order a Macallan '12' neat, single malt, all the time. It's just that more men drink Scotch."

Her voice took on a mild, "make my day" tone.

"Do you know how many men walk up to my bar and order a cosmopolitan?" she said.

THE VAMP

ADAPTED FROM THE FLATIRON LOUNGE

2 ounces Scotch
$\frac{1}{2}$ ounce orange liqueur
2 ounces orange juice
$\frac{1}{2}$ ounce fresh lemon juice
2 dashes of Angostura bitters

Shake all the ingredients and strain into a wineglass over ice. Garnish with a flamed orange peel.

Yield: 1 serving

AVERAGE JOE

Lucy Colada & Cocorita

I DIDN'T GO OUT LOOKING for coconut cocktails, I swear.

Acting on a tip about a margarita, I walked into Lucy Mexican Barbecue, a restaurant on East 18th Street in the Flatiron district. Actually, I walked into ABC Carpet and Home, the Cyndi-Lauperesque department store on Broadway, looking for Lucy, which is also a part of the store. You go through trinket-filled Tibet, Morocco and Provence on your way to Mexico, if you use this entrance.

Lucy itself is a kind of lounge and dining room with a 1970s Acapulco theme—white cotton upholstery, dark barn-plank wood-siding walls with candle sconces, white muslin–shaded hanging lamps. It looks like a Club Med designed by Luis Barragan, the Mexican minimalist. You feel there is a large swimming pool nearby, with chaises longues and browning people in thongs, that you just can't see. But, it's night. Lucy's bar is blackened concrete, with red and yellow glass brick inserts, fluorescently lighted from below.

The waitresses wear black, and have black hair, in keeping with the Mexican theme. Can they really hire that way? Most spoke beautiful Spanish to the bartender.

The specialty margarita, which involves strawberries, sounded similar to the house margarita served at Dos Caminos on Park Avenue South, another Mexican lounge in the neighborhood, so I tried a Lucy Colada, a cocktail from the frozen drinks part of the menu.

I know. Frozen drinks are bimbos. What is the cocktail version of a sexist remark? The Lucy Colada has coconut cream in it, too, to keep your self-respect from returning anytime soon. The bartender served it in a Mexican beanpot-shaped goblet; he floated the dark rum on the top of the cream-colored drink. You stir it in with a straw. It's dessert, but it's tasty. Passion fruit steels it up with acidity.

Half converted (or half loco), I ordered a Cocorita, which is a coconut margarita. Now I had a pair of shapely coconut cocktails with me at the bar, and happiness started to hit—"Average Joe" with tickets to Acapulco in his pocket.

"People are going to think you're the biggest drunk on Earth," the bartender said, without enough humor, I thought.

That's when Gwyneth Paltrow walked in. Gwyneth Paltrow No. 1. A white blonde, she faced the bar, put her bag down on the pastel, serape-striped barstool, opened it, picked up her cell phone, flipped it open and flipped it shut like someone checking a gun clip.

She said two things rapidly to the bartender: "I think I'll do white" and "What kind of Chardonnay?" She had her gold credit card down on the bar before the drink arrived. The tab was running. She looked at my unfinished drinks.

"That good, huh," she said.

It was 6:20. The bar was now crowded. I reached for my coat, parked on a stool.

"Are you leaving?" Ms. Paltrow asked and moved her bag to my stool.

That's when Gwyneth Paltrow walked in. Gwyneth Paltrow No. 2.

"Oh, my God," said Ms. Paltrow No. 1. "You're killing me. You're wearing the same thing as me." She was right, too—ribbed beige turtleneck, black trousers, white blond hair.

They looked like a pair of coconut cream cocktails.

Which, I have a very new respect for.

LUCY COLADA

ADAPTED FROM LUCY

2 ounces passion fruit puree
2 ounces Coco Lopez
1½ ounces Meyers's dark rum
2 cups ice cubes
Shaved coconut and diced fresh ripe mango

Place all the ingredients, except the coconut and mango, in a blender and blend at high speed for a short time. Strain into a chilled colada glass. Garnish with coconut and mango and serve with a straw.

Yield: 1 serving

COCORITA

ADAPTED FROM LUCY

2½ ounces tequila blanco
1½ ounces triple sec
1 teaspoon fresh lime juice
3 ounces Coco Lopez
2 cups ice cubes
Lime slice

Combine all the ingredients, except the lime, in a blender and blend until you have a frozen liquid. Pour into a hurricane cocktail glass. (For a thicker drink, omit a few ice cubes.) Garnish the rim with a lime slice.

Yield: 1 serving

MEN ABOUT TOWN

I WANT TO SEE THE WORLD

Sir Francis Drake, Huckleberry Ginn & Martin Luther

YOU'RE GOING TO HAVE TO TRUST ME ON THIS ONE.

The Sir Francis Drake, served at Hearth, a restaurant on East 12th Street, is a shot of sherry, topped off with Clamato juice. It's delicious.

Mike Mraz, the bar manager who invented it, has ten years of experience bartending, including "a bar in a dry county in Kansas," he said, but his specialty cocktail list for Hearth is a kind of prodigious first.

Included is the Huckleberry Ginn, a gin cooler with huckleberry syrup and ginger beer, and the Martin Luther—a gin martini with a wash of Bushmills Irish whiskey instead of vermouth. Mr. Mraz's directive from Paul Grieco, the general manager, who was formerly the service and wine director at Gramercy Tavern, and from Marco Canora, formerly the chef at Craft, was to create cocktails with three ingredients or fewer. That makes them perfect for adventurous home consumption.

The Sir Francis Drake, which is seasoned with celery salt, black pepper, Tabasco and freshly grated horseradish, tastes like a sherry and a tapa together in a glass. Mr. Mraz said he typically spent more time explaining the name than making the drink.

"He's the guy who defeated the Spanish Armada," Mr. Mraz said of

Sir Francis. "Part of the booty was sixteen thousand barrels of sherry, which is one of the reasons sherry became such a popular thing in England."

When I arrived last Friday night, the bar at Hearth was crowded with filthy wine drinkers—prosperous types who can take up two bar stools and not feel bothered to move. There were three women in dark day-to-evening suits who looked like editors at literary publishing houses: haircuts as opposed to hairdos, light makeup and small, sensible earrings—the fashion equivalent of political correctness.

Hearth's waiters wear Tommy Hilfiger striped dress shirts and new blue jeans. The long, low room, with a red ceiling and copper beams, a slate-floored bar at one end and a cork-floored dining room at the other, looks like a dining hall at a nice and expensive Northeastern prep school. Diners appeared to be in their early thirties or late forties, still game for a trip to the East Village if it involved a destination like a restaurant. Hearth, on Friday night, looked and sounded like a Groton reunion.

Sailing smoothly with Sir Francis, I circumnavigated the rest of the cocktail menu. The Huckleberry Ginn was part aperitif, part palate cleanser—a public television version of cocktail drinking and Twain. The Martin Luther nails you to the door. Mr. Mraz warned me about drinking it. I think that I am not spiritually (as in mixed drinks) rigorous enough for the Martin Luther.

I want to see the world, I thought as I finished my Sir Francis Drake, not leave it.

SIR FRANCIS DRAKE

ADAPTED FROM HEARTH

4 ounces Mott's Clamato juice
Dash each of celery salt, black pepper, Tabasco
and freshly grated horseradish
2 ounces Tío Pepe dry sherry
Lemon wedge

Mix the Clamato juice with the spices and seasonings. Pour the sherry into an 8-ounce glass filled with ice. Top off with the spiced Clamato juice and garnish with the lemon wedge.

Yield: 1 serving

HUCKLEBERRY GINN

ADAPTED FROM HEARTH

2 ounces gin
Splash of huckleberry syrup *(see Note)*
Splash of fresh lemon juice
Barritts Bermuda Stone ginger beer
Lemon twist

Fill an 8-ounce glass with ice; pour in the gin, splash in the huckleberry syrup and lemon juice, and fill to the brim with ginger beer. Garnish with the lemon twist.

Yield: 1 serving

Note: To make huckleberry syrup, cook berries and sugar together in a pan over medium heat. Use a ratio of sugar half the weight of the berries—for example, 1 pound berries to $1/2$ pound sugar. When liquefied to syrup, strain. (The berries can be used over pancakes or ice cream.)

MARTIN LUTHER

ADAPTED FROM HEARTH

1 ounce Bushmills Irish whiskey
5 ounces gin, chilled
Lemon twist

Swirl the whiskey in a martini glass to "wash" the sides. Add the gin.
Garnish with a lemon twist.

Yield: 1 serving

BLUE-EYED

The Incredible Hulk

LIL' KIM GOT THE NAME WRONG, but her fingernail extension was right on the mark.

"Imagine, ladies, you're out at like a picnic with your man," said Carson Daly, the host of *Last Call,* interviewing Lil' Kim, the rapper, on late-night television. "You got a little wine. Maybe a little Cristal, whatever your choice is."

Lil' Kim broke in.

"Nowadays, blue Hypnotize," she said.

"All *right,*" the audience free-styled.

What she meant is Hpnotiq, a blue, fruit-flavored, vodka-spiked Cognac beverage hatched like a Raëlian baby in France nineteen months ago to compete with Rémy Red and Alizé's three Passions and to capitalize on the phenomenal recent success of Cognac beverages in the United States. Nine and a half million 9-liter cases of Cognac and its blends were sold last year—an all-time high.

According to David Johnson, a psychologist writing about the effects of color, "Peaceful, tranquil blue causes the body to produce calming chemicals, so it is often used in bedrooms. Blue can also be cold and depressing. Fashion consultants recommend wearing blue to job interviews because it symbolizes loyalty. People are more productive in blue rooms. Studies show weightlifters are able to handle heavier weights in blue gyms."

Larry Kass, at Heaven Hill Distilleries in Bardstown, Kentucky, said of Lil' Kim's mistake, "Hey, we'll take it. What we have in place is the buzz about Hpnotiq. How do we repeat this formula in Little Rock?"

Heaven Hill, a large independent distiller, acquired Hpnotiq last month with the hope that it can bank on the blue-eyed bottle's club-scene cachet and push itself into the big time with Cognac's Big Three: Courvoisier, Hennessy and Rémy Martin.

Heaven Hill hired Nick Storm, too. Mr. Storm, who spent six years as a promoter at Sony Music, is the man who developed the original strategy to introduce the Hpnotiq (pronounced "hypnotic") brand.

"I applied my music background to a liquor background," Mr. Storm said. "Like breaking a record—instead of D.J.s, I used bartenders; in the Hamptons, then on the flip side, parties at urban events." Though he qualified "urban" by saying, "We know that urban is not black, white or Latino," Mr. Storm explained. "The buzz now is in the hip-hop and Latin markets."

At least 80 percent of the Cognac consumed domestically is drunk by African Americans, according to Rémy Martin, which welcomes with open wallets placements like music video appearances, where Cognac is an icon of wealth, health and happiness. Rémy has a new six-thousand-dollar bragging-rights bottle, Louis XIII Diamond, with a Baccarat crystal stopper that encases a 1.5-carat amber-colored diamond. Courvoisier has L'Esprit de Courvoisier—a five-thousand-dollar Lalique.

Alizé Passion, introduced in 1986, bombed when marketed to suburban women as a softer fruit spirit but bounced to life in a Tupac Shakur rap called "Thug Passion," and the rest is history.

Rhumba, a dance club on East Tremont Avenue in the Bronx, sponsors a weekly party, Hpnotiq Monday, which features seventy-five-dollar bottle sales and a cocktail called the Incredible Hulk, which is Cognac laced with Hpnotiq.

"You think guys won't drink it because ladies are drinking it," said Fernando Jurado, who attends the party. "But it's like contagion. One person at the bar orders it, and it spreads."

John Rivera, president of Prestige Entertainment, which originated

Hpnotiq Monday, said of his idea, "I like the color—the 'I Dream of Jeannie' type bottle."

"I've never tasted the drink," Mr. Rivera explained. "I drink wine."

THE INCREDIBLE HULK

ADAPTED FROM RHUMBA

1 ounce Hennessy
1 ounce Hpnotiq
3 maraschino cherries with stems

Fill a glass with ice. Pour the first layer, the Hennessy. Pour the second layer, the Hpnotiq. Garnish with the cherries and a sip stick.

Yield: 1 serving

EVERY MAN A KING

The Silver King

A HIGHBALL SOUNDS AS MUCH LIKE A DESCRIPTION of life at the top as it does a cocktail. And the presence of the Silver King on the menu at WD-50, Wylie Dufresne's new restaurant on Clinton Street on the Lower East Side, is perfectly appropriate. The drink, a version of a gin fizz, is an unofficial host to the low-riding hip hospitality of Mr. Dufresne's haute cuisine establishment.

On Wednesday evening, Bryan Ferry, the baby-boomer Bing Crosby, sang "Just One of Those Things" on a CD to young guests sitting at the lime-beige marble bar, drinking cocktails served on dryly self-conscious "WD-50" cardboard coasters and sharing plates of the thirty-two-year-old chef's immaculately stylish-looking food.

Everything is so finely balanced by suavity that it is like having an inner ear with more interesting friends than yours.

WD-50's two bartenders wore raw-indigo blue jeans and dark cherry shirts. The arriving clientele, with their flattened hair, small bowling-bag purses and mini trench coats, could have stepped out of a dressing trailer parked on Clinton Street and walked into the restaurant as a group.

The Silver King is a reinterpretation of a recipe published in the *Savoy Cocktail Book* in 1930. Devised by Eben Freeman, the bar manager, it is refreshing from head to toe, which is not an easy task. Not too sweet, not too strong, not too stupid, it has Goldilocks's gift for lottery, if the three bears had run a bar.

"It's for people who don't like gin," Mr. Freeman said. "There's not a predominant gin taste."

Lemon juice keeps it tart; soda water keeps it light; orange bitters keeps it smart.

The Silver King, like most fizzes, has an egg white in it, which froths when the cocktail is shaken, producing a "head" on the drink. Fizzes are a New Orleans invention that capitalized on the appearance of bottled soda water in the nineteenth century. Huey P. Long, governor of Louisiana from 1928 to 1932, is widely credited with popularizing them. Nicknamed the "Kingfish," Long campaigned for president on the slogan "Every man a king," demonstrating the fizz at a press event in New York.

The Silver King (no relation) is served in a highball glass or a tall Collins glass. WD-50 puts tiny straws in it, to avoid a milk mustache, and a vivid orange slice fits flatly into the top—a neat bit of modern design.

"Looks like an alien," said the bartender who served it, wiggling his fingers like antennae on either side of his lanky hair. "Are you a fan of Wylie's?" Mr. Dufresne, mutton-chopped and pony-tailed, was visible in the kitchen at the back, corralled like a quarterback by cooks, directing his food into the dining room.

No, I thought, as I drew the last ticklish sip from my glass. I'm here working.

THE SILVER KING

ADAPTED FROM WD-50

2 ounces gin
1 ounce fresh lemon juice
1 teaspoon simple syrup
4 dashes orange bitters
1 egg white
1 ounce soda water
Orange slice

Place all the ingredients except the soda water and orange slice in a cocktail shaker filled with ice. Shake until the egg white froths. Strain into a Collins glass filled with ice. Top with soda water and garnish with the slice of orange.

Yield: 1 serving

DEEP TISSUE

The Union Cocktail

LAST WEEK I WENT OUT LOOKING FOR SEX, and I found it.

At the bar at Pop Burger, a model-svelte, South Beach North–style burger joint in the meatpacking district, I ordered four house specials: the Pink Panty Pulldown, the Cosmopolitang, the Flirtini and the Union Cocktail—I'm assuming as in suit. Pop Burger, which has a take-out counter up front, has a lounge in the back—McDonald's with a velvet rope.

The bartender was a hustler. I started a tab with my American Express card, which I was bluntly asked to produce. It's a practice you don't find in bars that aren't turning drinks like tricks. You are in the presence of a cocktails equal sex bartender.

And frankly, that's not a bad thing if that's what you've come out for. Sex is a shot, like gin or vodka, and drinks have a blush-less and bold history of mood-producing—good and bad. You knock it back and you take your chances.

The Pink Panty Pulldown is a vanilla vodka and grenadine cocktail, and it is nasty. As I pulled at my Pink Panty, a bald man in heavy black eyeglasses tried to pick me up.

"Are you reviewing?" he asked, as I scribbled. "I review, too," he said engagingly.

Only in New York would someone try to pick you up because they thought you were a critic. It's emotional suicide, and the city is full of them. Just put a cocktail in your mouth and squeeze the trigger. And who empowered the Otto Preminger look?

There was a birthday party going on around us. It was the D.J. Bill Coleman's birthday. Balloons bobbed the blond-wood ceiling. Seventies and eighties music bobbed the crowd—late Diana Ross ("Upside Down"), KC and the Sunshine Band and other bands from the "uh huh uh huh" or "ow ow ow ow" era. Disco still has a desperate edge to it to hear—the Studio 54 into Xenon years when AIDS worked the party and only insiders knew it was there, like a VIP room celebrity, or how to meet it. Disco still sells sex, too, like cocktails, even when you're packing rubber.

When I asked for the Flirtini, then the Union Cocktail, the bartender broke into a smile. Whether it was honor among thieves or I busted a price barrier, like the right bill in a lapdancer's thong, we were agreeing to agree. Otto Preminger disappeared into the back room. Rosie Perez, the actor and a birthday guest, followed him in.

The Union Cocktail seemed less on the make, more interested in talking. It has tequila and cassis, which produces a pleasant thoughtfulness, though without worry, and lime to keep the conversation tart.

I ordered the Cosmopolitang last. Wetting them with an orange slice, the bartender rubbed the rim of the martini glass with his fingers—that's bar sex, what "body workers" call deep tissue in the ads. The Cosmopolitang is orange juice, and you could drink six before your brain started asking you questions. It's sex, too. You've spent the night and you've been invited to breakfast. Opt for the coffee shop. It's safer.

A blond-haired black woman to my left at the bar introduced herself. She had just met Ms. Perez, and with four cocktails sitting before me, I looked like another player. She was the D.J.'s mother, and the man next to her was her husband. They had driven from North Carolina for the evening.

Prince came up next on the turntables, the artist now known as the man who performed with Beyoncé at the 46th annual Grammy awards in February. He was covering his own song, "I Feel for You," which became a hit for Chaka Khan in 1984. By the 1990s, what epidemiologists characterized as AIDS's "second decade," seriological experts noted that the HIV prevalence rate started rising at age twelve, and continued to rise through teenage years. Excusing myself from Mr. and Mrs. Coleman, I started to reach for my Cosmopolitang, to finish it, then asked for the check instead.

No thanks, I decided. Let's just be friends.

THE UNION COCKTAIL

ADAPTED FROM POP BURGER

1¹⁄₂ ounces Herradura Hacienda del Cristero Blanco tequila
³⁄₄ ounce Cointreau
1 ounce fresh lime juice
¹⁄₂ ounce simple syrup or 3 teaspoons sugar
Lime twist

Fill a shaker with ice. Add the tequila, Cointreau, lime juice, and syrup or sugar. Shake well. Strain into a chilled martini glass. Garnish with a twist of lime.

Yield: 1 serving

SOPHISTICATION HAS ITS COSTS

Bleeding Heart, Calamansi Collins & Jefferson Bloody Mary

IF THERE ARE REWARDS TO LIVING in twenty-first-century New York (there have got to be some, right?), they are places like Simpson Wong's seven-seat bar at his restaurant, Jefferson, at 121 West 10th Street.

Mr. Wong's bar is the soul of the new machine, for a cocktail culture entering its next, very different golden age. It is characterized by the quality of a casual experience, not social ritual: cashmere replacing silk.

The black leather stools at the white French oak bar face the dining room, not a wall of bottles, over a low opaque glass backsplash. People drinking can watch people eating, like a droll illustration come to life in an urbane magazine. It is an immensely satisfying kind of quiet camaraderie: the fun of being an adult with enough money in your pocket for a nine-dollar cocktail and the ambience of a beautifully engineered room.

Jefferson was designed by Philip Wu, one of Mr. Wong's four partners. Like the friendly, civil bartenders, it is deferential to a fault— a wall of oak, a wall of glass and a slatted wall and ceiling, punctuated by horizontal strips of light, that give the impression you are sitting inside an elegant corrugated box. Something you would buy at a Japanese stationery store, without a clue why.

Mr. Wong, the chef, with his manager, Roger Kugler, created the cocktail menu, which was introduced on Monday. It includes the Jefferson Bloody Mary, an Asian tomato juice drink, the Calamansi Collins, with calamansi juice, and the Bleeding Heart, a double-rum drink that takes advantage of blood oranges now in the market. Mr. Wong said the season was late; he buys his fruit at Whole Foods on Seventh Avenue at 24th Street, like anybody else.

The Bleeding Heart, served like a punch in a highball glass, is also subtle and stylish. Mr. Wong intends it to work well with food. The drink is the color of a twenty-three-dollar lipstick. The cocktail's name is a reference to its blood-orange ingredient. Mr. Wong has his eye on Valentine's Day, too.

Last Valentine's Day, he recalled, a man broke up with his girl-friend, who was pregnant, at their table in the restaurant, and at several other tables people proposed. Sophistication has its costs.

Asked if he himself is romantically happy, Mr. Wong answered instead that he was "really busy" professionally. Sad?

"Stressed," he said on his cell phone while shopping in Chinatown on Thursday morning.

In previous lives, before his career as a restaurateur, Mr. Wong worked with *Penthouse* magazine, when it tried unsuccessfully to publish in China. Mr. Wong, who is Chinese-Malaysian, speaks Chinese. He has also worked at the United Nations with the World Meteorological Organization. He learned how to cook from his mother, who cooked for the workers at his father's lumberyard company on the east coast of Malaysia.

Mr. Wong's heart might not bleed, but it's in the right place. His new cocktail is as sympathetic as the restaurant you drink it in, interesting, not overwhelming, entertaining without condescension. You feel its accomplishment is yours alone. And in this city, that's what reward is all about.

BLEEDING HEART

ADAPTED FROM JEFFERSON

1 ounce white rum
1 ounce dark (or gold) rum
$^1/_2$ ounce Cointreau or triple sec
Juice of 1 lime wedge
4 ounces blood orange juice
Orange, lime and tangerine wedges

Shake all the liquid ingredients together with ice and strain into an 8-ounce highball glass filled with crushed ice. For the garnish, thread two skinned tangerine or orange wedges on each of two wooden skewers. Run skewers, crossing, through a lime wedge.

Yield: 1 serving

CALAMANSI COLLINS

ADAPTED FROM JEFFERSON

2 ounces gin
1 ounce calamansi juice
$^3/_4$ ounce fresh lemon juice
$^1/_2$ ounce fresh lime juice
Club soda

Stir all the ingredients, except club soda, with ice. Strain into a Collins glass filled three-quarters full with fresh ice and top off with club soda.

Yield: 1 serving

JEFFERSON BLOODY MARY

ADAPTED FROM JEFFERSON

4 ounces fresh tomato juice
2 ounces vodka
$1/_2$ teaspoon wasabi paste
(mix wasabi powder with just enough water to make a thick, dough-like paste)
$1/_4$ teaspoon each of freshly grated horseradish and ginger
2 dashes of Tabasco
1 dash of Worcestershire sauce *(white or brown)*
Juice of 1 lemon wedge *(from $1/_8$ lemon)*
$1/_8$ teaspoon each sea salt, celery salt and
freshly ground black pepper
Lemongrass stalk
Cucumber slice
Lime wedge

Shake the ingredients, except the lemongrass, cucumber and lime, with ice. Strain into a highball glass with fresh ice. Garnish with lemongrass, cucumber and lime.

Yield: 1 serving

A PRIZEFIGHTER AROUND CHILDREN

The Bone

The Chickenbone Cafe is now history. The Bone lives on, history in the making.

IF YOU WANT TO GET A MAN TO DO SOMETHING, dare him to do it. I would say that's the operational theory behind the Bone, the house drink at the Chickenbone Cafe on the south side of Williamsburg, in Brooklyn.

The Bone, shaken with ice and served straight up in a tall, thin shot glass, is rye whiskey, lime juice, a little sugar and several muscular dashes of Tabasco sauce. It sounds like a chest-hair cocktail.

"It took me a while to get around to trying it, let's put it that way," said the Bone's inventor, David Wondrich. Mr. Wondrich, who writes about cocktails, advised Zak Pelaccio, the cafe's chef and a friend, on the drinks list.

You can imagine the Chickenbone's art-community patrons mixing at the bar with the "locals" (art-community people like to do that) and downing a couple of Bones, shouting "Break a bone!" before they knock each fiery cannonball back.

"Dave came over to my house one night, and we basically played around with booze for a while," Mr. Pelaccio said. "We definitely had a few. We figured doing the martini thing was overplayed, so we concentrated on the darker liquors. You have this image of the south side being harder, grungier—not pink drinks out of martini glasses. We wanted something a little more butch."

Mr. Wondrich said that he got the idea for rye whiskey dosed with Tabasco sauce from a book of hard-luck stories, *Tales of the Ex-Tanks,* which purports to be the "minutes" of the Harlem Club of Former Alcoholic Degenerates, written by Clarence Louis Cullen, a *New York Sun* reporter, and published in 1900.

As if the Bone didn't have enough testosterone on its own, the bar menu offers the Bone With Beef—a side of smoked beef with chilies to chase it. That's a sex change, not a cocktail.

"God, it's such an intense drink—it's nice to match it with something," Mr. Pelaccio said. "My wife's Yugoslavian and we spend time in Astoria eating Yugoslavian food. There's a woman with a little grocery on 30th Street who keeps pieces of dried beef hanging overhead—*suvo meso.*"

But the bad Bone has a big secret. It's a pussycat when met, like a prizefighter around children. In its $2^1/_4$-ounce glass, the cocktail comes on like a slugger, but it's gentle at heart. Because of the lime juice and sugar, it will dance you affectionately around the ring before it knocks you out.

The waiter who served me a Bone on Wednesday night said the drink is popular, in part, because it's also "the cheapest thing on the menu." Stingers and daiquiris are eight dollars—the Bone weighs in at six dollars. Mr. Pelaccio said the cafe shares the building with rehearsal studios. Musicians stop in between late-night sets and split the difference in price with "a Bone and a two-dollar Pabst."

Mr. Wondrich, its creator, advised getting the cocktail as cold as possible, then straining it—and shooting.

"It's to be consumed quickly," he said, as though he were describing something experimental. "It's not a four-sipper."

What's the matter, guy? Scared?

THE BONE

ADAPTED FROM THE CHICKENBONE CAFE

2 ounces Wild Turkey rye
1 teaspoon fresh lime juice
$^3/_4$ teaspoon superfine sugar
2 dashes of Tabasco sauce

Mix all the ingredients in a cocktail shaker with ice. Shake well. Strain and serve straight up in a shot glass.

Yield: 1 serving

A FOUR-OUNCE EDUCATION

Ginger Daiquiri

"BUT HER SOCIAL AGENDA WAS ZERO," said the man sitting next to me at Mas, a restaurant on Downing Street in the West Village. "So we didn't give her any money."

Sometimes you want to go out for a drink, not to meet friends, as this gentleman had, but to have a quiet moment to yourself and to observe this great city. A cocktail can be an occasion to dip into other people's lives, and to reflect upon your own, in the gentlest possible manner. It can be a four-ounce education, a gifted entertainment or the cheapest kind of date.

Mas's little bar and lounge area is a pretty perfect place to do this. It looks out a large window onto the street, with benches below to sit and take in the view. And the ginger daiquiri, a house specialty with a fresh ginger theme, is a perfectly paced drink for the exercise—not too fast, not too slow, a long, lovely descent, like an evening's light in May.

"I'm talking to Coca-Cola, and that's my dream," said the man next to me to his group, a cocktail in front of each of them.

Everything about Mas has been almost obsessively considered, which is fine, when you're keeping company with one of their cocktails, which wear the attention well. The details of the small establishment—the parchment lighting, the suavely suited owners, the casual correctness that informs the seasonal menu and the ambience too—are just more conversation to be overheard as you sit and drink. Mas, which is "farmhouse" in French and which is French American in intention, is like a tasteful apartment or a tasteful auberge where you and your cocktail might be staying as guests. It values its accent—the one that shares the knowledge, with a subtle smile and soft eye contact, that you've *lived* there too.

Mas is also proudly American. The bartender working on Wednesday, Andrew Hunter, curly-headed and all-American, could have been playing John Adams in a college production of *1776*. (A server walked by with a black spike Mohawk. He must be playing the natives. It's the West Village, isn't it?) And the ginger daiquiri, which Mr. Hunter developed with Thomas Wilson, an owner, has Meyer lemon juice in it (as well as Cointreau), a citrus fruit popularized by new American chefs.

Responding to a comment about the weight of the tree-stump stools in the lounge, Mr. Hunter explained that they were cut down and polished from a butternut tree in Mr. Wilson's father's backyard in Massachusetts. I pushed on mine heavily to face the bar and give my neighbors more privacy.

"You can chat with us if you like," said the man next to me, concerned that I was alone with a drink and appeared to be listening to my own thoughts.

"You're not a reporter, are you?"

GINGER DAIQUIRI

ADAPTED FROM MAS

Orange peel

Ginger sugar *(seal 6 ounces turbinado sugar with 1 ounce
fresh gingerroot in a jar for a week; shake the jar every day)*

2 ounces white Haitian rum

$1/2$ ounce Cointreau

$1/2$ ounce Meyers lemon juice

$1/2$ ounce ginger-infused simple syrup *(simple syrup macerated with peeled
fresh gingerroot; 4 ounces ginger will yield one pint; macerate two days)*

Swipe the orange peel on the rim of a cocktail glass; press the wet
rim down into a shallow dish of the ginger sugar to "frost" the rim.
Combine the remaining ingredients in a shaker with ice; shake and
strain into the glass to the rim. Garnish with peel.

Yield: 1 serving

DR. BROWN

Wolf's Royal Cream Soda & The Harrison Tonic

ONE OF NEW YORK'S NEWEST COCKTAIL LOUNGES is not exactly where you would expect it to be: Chelsea or Williamsburg or the Lower East Side. It's in Wolf's Delicatessen on 57th Street, near the Avenue of the Americas, upstairs above the sandwich counter and the dessert case.

Wolf's unveiled a new menu last week (the items from the old dog-eared brown one reprinted on coffee-shop gloss stock), but now alongside the smoked fish platters and latkes is a cocktail list that includes house specialties like Wolf's Royal Cream Soda. That's Dr. Brown's Cream Soda, a deli staple, with Absolut vodka in it.

The lounge, which also serves breakfast (the bar's bottle shelves rotate to conceal the liquor), is the latest update to Wolf's, which is owned by Ralph Scotto, who trademarked the name in 1998 and moved the deli to its present location. The original Wolf's, at the corner, was started in 1951 by Dave Wolf, a concentration camp survivor, as one of a small chain of delis in Manhattan.

"People keep saying, 'Well, you're Italian, how do you do Jewish?' " Mr. Scotto, an Italian American from Brooklyn, said on Wednesday. Mr. Scotto was wearing a Big Ralph's Brake Shop baseball cap and a Ducati shirt.

"I come from a cooking family," he explained. "It's a cuisine. This is what I do. I don't do pizza."

Mr. Scotto, fifty-five, has been in the deli business since he was eleven.

"My father broke his neck diving into a swimming pool," he recalled. "I took a bus to 86th Street, and there was a delicatessen called Hy Tulip. I walked up to the door. Marty Sachs, the owner, was throwing his dishwasher out. He gave me an apron, and I worked in the kitchen next to the guys making knishes."

Over the years, in various delis, Mr. Scotto explained, he learned how to cook corned beef and pastrami. He can also "pump" tongue—a method of curing beef tongue by putting a needle into the artery and injecting it with brine until it swells.

The intention at Wolf's is to make it an "upscale deli," as Mr. Scotto put it, an idea that might strike Wolf's regulars as making as much sense as a downscale Hotel Plaza. You still get a bowl of pickles and a bowl of coleslaw on the table with every meal. You still get tiny red-haired women, folded over like wallets, eating dinner at four in the afternoon. This is a cosmopolitan crowd, as in emigre, not as in Sarah Jessica Parker.

But cocktails are part of the plan. Wolf's Royal Cream Soda is good, if you like cream soda (I do). For the record, it's kosher, too. The production of Absolut is supervised by Rabbi Moshe Edelmann in Sweden. Dr. Brown's Cream Soda, which originated in 1869 in Williamsburg, Brooklyn, bears the KOF-K certificate of rabbinical supervision. Dr. Brown's drinks, including cherry soda and Cel-Ray Soda, a seltzer produced with celery seed, were most popular in Jewish delis before Coca-Cola became kosher, early in the 1930s.

And if you're going to eat dinner at four, there's nothing wrong in my book with pushing the cocktail hour back to three.

WOLF'S ROYAL CREAM SODA

ADAPTED FROM WOLF'S DELICATESSEN

1¼ ounces Absolut Vanilia
5 ounces Dr. Brown's Cream Soda
Lime slice

Pour the vodka into a wineglass filled with ice. Pour cream soda over that; don't stir. Garnish with the lime slice.

Yield: 1 serving

MEANWHILE, DOWNTOWN AT THE HARRISON, on the corner of Harrison and Greenwich Streets in TriBeCa, the bar is serving the Harrison Tonic, a house drink based on bourbon and Dr. Brown's Cel-Ray Soda.

Bourbon you know. Cel-Ray Soda is celery soda. At some point this was someone's idea of a healthy drink—the taste you can't identify and that you can't decide you like or want to spit out—hence Harrison's tonic: a nice spin on cocktail history and Catskills fresh-air camp culture.

But bourbon and a squeeze of lemon give the soda's vegetal flavor a subtlety that would have surprised Dr. Brown. It's a whiskey Collins, which is mixed with club soda, but less anemic. Papa—the kid's gonna live!

The Harrison, which is owned by Jimmy Bradley, the executive chef, and Danny Abrams, a team who also own the Red Cat in Chelsea and the Mermaid Inn in the East Village, is a kind of New-Age American tavern—dark wood and white wainscotting and shaded wall lamps, executed minimally and as more of a knowing reference to trusty, neighborhood spots and casual fine dining than as a complete ambience. The restaurant's logo, in a democratically fancy script, looks on its calling card like the herald of a "good" restaurant tucked into the steepled hills of rural Connecticut, a place you might have put on your cocktail clothes to motor to with other married couples in 1949. But it is another postwar era to be found here.

Mr. Bradley and Mr. Abrams opened the Harrison in October 2001, a month after the World Trade Center attack. The restaurant is eight blocks away from Ground Zero, and during its first years of operation, the sky outside its dark, suave interior was lighted white with klieg lights, like a convocation of ghosts.

The bar enjoys a financial crowd from the financial districts downtown, and even on Tuesday night, three years later, there was a tentative quality to the loudness and camaraderie of the young traders in shirt sleeves drinking there, ordering Grey Goose, the vodka of the hour, on the rocks, or showing their colleagues perfect form with a martini with a twist. If the gods of fortune and making good money have allowed them to be there, drinking after a fourteen-hour day, other gods have allowed it, too—the gods who could again blacken the blue sky and turn night white with sorrow.

There was "E-Z" guitar and lightly swinging organ music playing, and the bartender, with his mustache and necktie and knee-length apron, looked like William H. Macy in a Joel and Ethan Coen film. But there is not the safety that there used to be in memories, when nostalgia itself seems broken in half. In its place is before and after.

What you can do is reinvent, which the Harrison Tonic does neatly, celery soda and all. If it is a healthy drink, it is healthy in its optimism, that you can take any of the old ingredients and make something new. Unimpeachably so.

THE HARRISON TONIC

ADAPTED FROM THE HARRISON

1 1/2 ounces Maker's Mark bourbon
Dr. Brown's Cel-Ray Soda
Lemon wedge

Pour Maker's Mark into a rocks glass filled with ice and top with Dr. Brown's Cel-Ray. Garnish with a lemon wedge.

Yield: 1 serving

REVIVED

DRINK IT WHILE IT'S LAUGHING AT YOU

Southside

I WAS TURNED DOWN BY SOME OF THE MOST EXCLUSIVE clubs on the East Coast last month. I was trying to find a recipe for the Southside cocktail.

"We don't provide information to nonmembers," said the incredibly terse woman who answered the telephone at the Piping Rock Club in Locust Valley, New York.

Even for the purposes of a newspaper cocktail column?

"Especially not for that purpose," she explained. Click.

Ditto the Tokeneke Beach Club in Darien, Connecticut.

"We prefer privacy," said the suave gatekeeper who answered the phone. "We try to be as quiet and peaceful as possible." Soft click.

A cocktail that won't give an interview!

The Southside, a gin lemonade that is baptismal-font water to the traditional East Coast society set, is most typically a spring and summer refreshment, but as Bruce Snyder, the restaurant manager at the '21' Club, which did business with me, observed, "The spigot never shuts." That means, according to Mr. Snyder's thirty-six years of experience with his clientele, you retire the white shoes, straw hats, linen and seersucker on Labor Day, but the Southside sails on through, brisk autumn seas ahead. Dark rum, substituting occasionally for gin, relieves any boredom.

With its jockey theme, gentleman receptionist and drinking-cartoon Bar Room, the '21' Club, a former speakeasy on East 52nd Street, is a touchstone for the particularly metropolitan idea of a restaurant with a tacit membership—the only survivor of a saloon-society heyday that included the Stork Club and El Morocco.

After two previous addresses, '21' moved to 52nd Street in 1929, when it was called Jack and Charlie's. Fifty-second Street was called "Swing Street" during Prohibition, and the block between Fifth and Sixth Avenues, where '21' lives, was called the "wettest block on the street."

In last Sunday's episode of *Sex and the City*, the now mortal Mr. Big met with Carrie Bradshaw at '21' for a steak and a private talk in much the manner that J. J. Hunsecker in *Sweet Smell of Success* and Addison DeWitt in *All About Eve* also enjoyed the publicity of '21's privilege.

Steak house tablecloths and monogrammed hotel silver pepper mills dress the tables—a kind of old-money upscale-downscale. Every preppie I ever knew went to '21' on AWOL weekends in New York and tried to get served at the bar. Many succeeded. Many return as tourists with their families. With its toy-festooned ceiling, the '21' Bar Room is a hallowed birthday hall for boys who will become their fathers.

The Southside has the easy fit of a child's signet ring. Not adult like a cocktail, but two ounces of responsibility nevertheless. The fresh mint is a reality check in what could otherwise be a lemonade. Liberals make it with lime. A Southside Fizz is topped with seltzer, like a bromide.

"Drink it while it's laughing at you," bartenders are fond of saying.

In the right drinking circles, that's humor that passes for dry.

SOUTHSIDE

ADAPTED FROM THE '21' CLUB

2 ounces gin or dark rum
Juice of ¹/₂ lemon
Sugar to taste
Fresh mint leaves

Combine the ingredients in a shaker with ice and shake. Strain into a double old-fashioned glass filled with ice and garnish with a sprig of mint.

Yield: 1 serving

SHORTLY AFTER WE PUBLISHED THE COLUMN on the Southside, I received a handwritten letter at the newspaper, from S. Scott Nicholls, Jr., who lives on the Upper East Side.

It read:

Re: Shaken and Stirred, An East Coast Lubricant.

Some thirty-odd years ago, I learned how to make Southside mix, oftentimes incorrectly referred to as a "marinade."

I had a large mint patch outside my kitchen door that flourished every spring without any help, just as weeds and crabgrass sprout to our dismay. I was determined to ascertain the recipe for the "mix," and here is what I found.

Take a half gallon glass container with a screw-on cap and squeeze enough lemons to fill it two-thirds of the way to the top. Add sugar for the "to taste" and stir vigorously. Then insert enough mint to bring the level of the lemon juice to the top. Screw on the cap and place the container in your refrigerator for seventy-two hours. After three days, the mint has turned black. Remove the jar from your refrigerator and drain off the "mix." Discard the blackened mint. Take a highball glass filled with ice cubes two-thirds to the top, add two ounces of dark rum (Mt. Gay seems to be the most popular), vodka or gin. A garnish of fresh mint looks attractive but does not add anything to the flavor.

A Southside Fizz is only promoted by establishments that want to conserve their "mix." Also, some establishments will use crushed ice, mint leaves and rum (with lemon juice) and blend in a blender. This is also unsatisfactory, as the crushed ice immediately melts and leaves one with the impression that one is drinking a watered-down lemonade. Also, the task of removing tiny bits of mint from your tongue detracts from the enjoyment. Another important hint: do not take shortcuts. To save time, some clubs will use frozen lemon juice or lemonade. Any purist who knows the real thing will spot it immediately. Rather than embarrass their host or hostess, he or she will say nothing. But the next time they are invited, he or she will probably order a gin and tonic.

Many years ago, I was told that there was a club on the south shore of Long Island called the Southside Club (which no longer exists). I have never been able to ascertain if this was the origin of the Southside cocktail.

Sincerely,

S. Scott Nicholls, Jr.

Thank you, Mr. Nicholls, and cheers.

THERE'S THAT MUSIC AGAIN

Mojito

YOU CAN DRINK A MOJITO without really thinking about it, and that's a pretty good recommendation for a summer cocktail.

Then the music starts—the sad, swaying strum that seems to be coming out of a decaying Cuban guitar being played by a decaying Cuban guitar player with a soft voice and a gold tooth. But it's coming out of you. That's something to think about.

Succeeding the daiquiri and the Cuba libre, this year's round of arcaded Latin nostalgia is being distilled quickly in the mojito, with its gentle memory of rum, lime and mint. People at bars, including Cuban-themed restaurants like Asia de Cuba and Cuba Cafe in New York, are ordering them left and right. And liquor companies, seizing the mojito's moment, have introduced mojito-flavored rums like Mojito Club and Martí Auténtico: in effect, the "Buena Vista Social Club" in a bottle.

The mojito is also being knocked off and reinvented—the sincerest form of flattery. Douglas Rodríguez, the Latino celebrity chef, serves a mojito martini at Chicama in New York—a two-fisted attempt to grab two trends at once. Mary's Off Jane, a New York café, bakes mojito cookies.

"We developed a mojito product to tap into the trend," said Angelo Vassallo, a vice president at Pernod Ricard USA, which introduced Mojito Club last month. "The trend today is things Latino. The Latino experience is dictating fashion in drink. Clubs, prestige accounts were making their own mojitos."

Mr. Vassallo added, "We saw it as an opportunity to come up with a new flavor system, the next adopted by Americans—an alternative to the margarita, which is the number one cocktail in the country."

The mojito originated in Cuba as a farmers' drink in the late nineteenth century as Cuba's rum industry modernized, making the mojito as common as beer. Only the rich drank it with ice and soda. The mojito's popularity in the United States coincides with an increased interest in Cuban-style rums. Cuban rums are unavailable.

Joseph Magliocco, president of Chatham Imports, which developed Martí Auténtico, worked with two rum makers in the Dominican Republic to create his basic rum recipe, which emphasizes the notes of flower, fruit and nut that are typical of Cuban rums.

"It's a pre-Castro Cuban-style rum," Mr. Magliocco said. "We use a little hit of Caribbean cane sugar."

Yerba buena, or Cuban mint, specified in recipes as the mojito's native mint, is peppermint, though the classification is also loosely applied in Cuba to bergamot and the rugose form of spearmint, according to Dr. Art Tucker from the Department of Agriculture and Natural Resources at Delaware State University. Dr. Tucker is an expert on mint.

"The latter, *M. Spicata,* is very interesting and is found wherever the Spanish went, from Lake Atitlan in Guatemala to New Mexico to the Philippines," he said.

Ah, there's that music again.

MOJITO

ADAPTED FROM CUBA CAFE

1 ounce mint leaves, torn in half
2 ounces fresh lime juice
1¹/₂ ounces white rum
1 teaspoon superfine sugar
Crushed ice
4 ounces club soda
Lime wedge

Muddle the mint with the lime juice in the bottom of a tall cocktail glass. Add the rum, sugar, crushed ice and soda. Cover and shake, and uncover, serving with a lime wedge.

Yield: 1 serving

A SUPERB CHILL

That Stinger

That Bar is now a clam shack restaurant with a new ownership. That's that.

WITH THE SOCIAL SEASON AND THE HOLIDAYS headed into high gear, there are likely to be nights when you'll want a cocktail at the end of the evening as much as at the beginning.

My suggestion is a stinger, a Prohibition-era cocktail as classic as the Chrysler Building. Most agree it is one of the few cocktails that will also qualify as an after-dinner drink, though it's no Kahlúa on ice cream, either. Its nickname is the "nightcap cocktail."

Evelyn Waugh, the British author of *Brideshead Revisited,* and more important, the author of *Vile Bodies,* in which one character, Miles Malpractice, describes a rough Channel crossing as "exactly like being inside a cocktail shaker," drank stingers as a "signature."

The stinger is tricky: two ingredients only, brandy and white crème de menthe. It's all in the proportion. Go heavy on the brandy, though not light on the liqueur, and use the best brandy you can comfortably write off in a mixed drink. The stinger can also be built on vodka, which gives you a cocktail more contemporary in taste; on tequila, which transforms it into a sophistication from a shot; or on bourbon, which gives you a Dixie stinger. (There's got to have been at least one exotic dancer who worked under that name.)

Period wisdom was that the arctic sweetness of the cream mint disguised the mouth boil of bootleggers' booze.

But even legally, the stinger brings breathtaking refreshment to a hard-liquor cocktail, one that wakes you up like a bright idea and makes you think for a minute or two that you're actually smarter than you are. That's my idea of an intelligent drink, and the stinger's not a bad choice to start an evening with either, if it's confidence you seek in your cocktails.

A few things will get you into trouble quickly. Resist green crème de menthe (yes, it's an Irish stinger, and no, it's not a distinction worth making, even if it's Christmas colored). The drink looks suave when it's invisible, like Cary Grant and Constance Bennett in *Topper,* and shows more satisfying menace when sipped.

Resist garnishes, unless you're presenting a tray of stingers at a party, and you can't help yourself. The drinks are festive, it's true, and to be fair, a large part of the popularity of cocktails has always been the "silly" factor, from napkins ("I hope my ship comes in before my dock rots") to shakers and swizzles (penguins, monkeys).

That Bar, at 116 Smith Street in Brooklyn, serves a perfectly proportioned stinger with a green-dyed-sugar rim and a mint chocolate, which reminds me of one of the few things that I've learned in life: only beautiful people can get away with ugly clothes.

Start out simply, with a standard martini glass and lots of ice. A superb chill accelerates the mint and refines the brandy. And don't worry about that bottle of white crème de menth taking up space at your bar.

The "dirty girl scout" calls for it, too.

THAT STINGER

2 ounces brandy or vodka
1 ounce white crème de menthe
Andes chocolate mint candy, optional *(most bars don't do this)*

Combine the brandy or vodka with crème de menthe in a chilled glass and stir. Garnish with mint candy.

Yield: 1 serving

A MORNING DRINK

The Manhattan

"THE SUMMERS WERE FUN IN NEW YORK," wrote John O'Hara in *Butterfield 8*, his speakeasy novel about Gloria Wandrous, a socialite call girl whose last sip of life was suicide off the side of a boat.

"Planter's punches. Mint juleps. Tom Collinses. Rickeys. You had two or three of these to usher in the season, and paid a visit or two to the beer places, and then you went back to whiskey and water," O'Hara observed. "What was the use of kidding yourself?"

When O'Hara published his liquid-diet classic in 1935, New York was a whiskey town, rye whiskey in particular.

Whiskey has always been a hard-core idea as well as a drink—neat, straight up, on the rocks—but it is occasionally a civilized one, too, and the manhattan is the closest that whiskey has come to acting cultivated in a cocktail crowd.

Butterfield 8 is back in print, and New York is becoming a whiskey town again. New Yorkers are rediscovering the manhattan.

"We've been serving a lot of manhattans lately," said Joshua Wallin, the bar manager at Morgans Bar at Morgans hotel on Madison Avenue between 37th and 38th Streets. "You start off drinking sweet drinks when you're young. As people get older, they develop a taste for alcohol. You still have those traditional drinkers out there, and I think whiskey has caught on with a younger crowd."

Mr. Wallin serves his manhattan with bourbon whiskey, not rye as it was served during its "red-hot minute" at the Stork Club, in the words of Lucius Beebe in his *Stork Club Bar Book* of 1946. Mr. Beebe listed the manhattan, the first recipe in his book, as a morning drink, to be drunk before noon "because of its unrivaled tonic qualities as a restorative and element for firming the moral fiber."

Popular tastes have changed the standard manhattan, invented in the late nineteenth century, into a bourbon drink, most bartenders agree, with sweet vermouth and a maraschino cherry or twist of lemon.

Expert bartenders will make the distinction between a manhattan, a "perfect" manhattan, which is a mix of sweet and dry vermouths, and a "dry" manhattan, which uses dry vermouth instead of sweet.

Mr. Wallin likes to make his manhattans with Maker's Mark. A word to the wise, though, about naming your brand when ordering a manhattan.

"The most exciting manhattan is one compounded with ordinary-quality bar whiskey rather than the rarest overproof article," Mr. Beebe wrote.

It's the kind of snide class war in a glass that would have made O'Hara gargle with glee.

THE MANHATTAN

ADAPTED FROM MORGANS BAR
AT MORGANS HOTEL

Bitters
2¹/₂ ounces Maker's Mark bourbon *(or rye if you prefer)*
1 ounce sweet vermouth
Maraschino cherry or lemon twist

Shake one or two drops of bitters into a cocktail glass, gently twisting the glass from side to side. Shake out the excess, leaving only the residue. Mix bourbon or rye with sweet vermouth in a mixing glass. Add ice. Shake well. Strain the contents into a cocktail glass. Garnish with cherry or lemon.

Yield: 1 serving

GLOBAL POSITIONING

The Sidecar

HERE'S A DRINK THAT HAS IT ALL. You would date this drink. And not wait a day to call it.

The sidecar has three ingredients—perfect ingredients. Cognac, Cointreau, freshly squeezed lemon juice—when you make it right, you get a 10, maybe a 12. Tasted, the sidecar's sweet-to-sour sway, and back again, has the smart, sublime balance of a Zen riddle, served in a sleek glass.

With its suede rose color and serious spirit content, men can drink it and feel like men, women can drink it and feel like women. Couples can equate.

For cocktail-culture devotees, there's a neat starched-cuff scuffle about who invented the sidecar. The Ritz's Little Bar and Harry's New York Bar both claim it, in Paris, in the 1920s. Harry's owner, Harry MacElhone, concocted it, says John J. Poister, author of *The New American Bartender's Guide*. Mr. MacElhone served hot dogs with martinis, too.

Whoever or wherever, the sidecar watched the martini, popularized in the 1930s, grow up.

Now resurgent, the sidecar is a subtle spokesman for a second wave of interest in classic cocktails, a Prohibition-era relic being re-created for recent New Yorkers in East Village bars like Angel's Share, on Stuyvesant Street, a speakeasy behind an unmarked door in a second-floor Japanese noodle house. Angel's Share is one of several bars in the city where young bartenders pride themselves on purveying the classics, as intended, as repositories of cocktail culture.

And drinks like the sidecar, with its jazz age heritage of a kind of mannerly mayhem, have been preserved for those who remember them in uptown hotel bars like the Cafe Pierre at the Pierre.

"Most people these days ordering sidecars have been turned on to them," said Connor Coffey, the beverage director at the Red Cat, a bar and restaurant in Chelsea in New York. "It's not a drink they've seen on *Sex and the City*."

The key to the sidecar is fresh lemon juice, which keeps it bright. Asked if he could make a sidecar and asked if he used fresh lemon juice, Eben Freeman, the happy-dog bartender on duty at the Red Cat last Sunday, said "of course," twice. Use lemonade or sours mix, and the drink's a cookie.

"Would you like a sugar rim, sir?" asked Richard Weyant, the bartender at the Cafe Pierre that same night.

For purists and/or fetishists, the sidecar has, as every great drink should, a point of honor, to be decided on a personal basis by those who drink it. Does the glass have a sugar rim, swiped with a lemon wedge and dusted with sugar, or is it presented plain? (Connoisseurs use confectioners' sugar.)

The real issue is in being asked. Like any classic cocktail, the sidecar, in this day and age, is at its greatest use as a Global Positioning System. If you find yourself in a place where they don't know the question, then they can't make the answer.

You're not in a place that will support life.

THE SIDECAR

ADAPTED FROM CAFE PIERRE

1$^{1}/_{2}$ ounces Courvoisier
$^{3}/_{4}$ ounce Cointreau
$^{1}/_{2}$ ounce fresh lemon juice

Shake the ingredients with ice. Strain into a glass. For a sugar rim, swipe the rim with a lemon wedge; dab with sugar.

Yield: 1 serving

ASIA MAJOR, AND AN ATOLL

A CONSUMMATE DIPLOMAT

Tablatini

I ALMOST KILLED A COUPLE OF FRIENDS a few years back by serving what I called a Moroccan martini. It was a vodka martini with lemon conserve in it instead of vermouth. Lemon conserve is made traditionally in Morocco, to accompany grilled meats, by steeping lemons in coarse salt. The saline content in my martini could have floated a potato.

But mistakes like mine haven't discouraged bars in New York from similar experiments. The popularity of "fusion cooking," which combines tastes and techniques from disparate cuisines (the Fusion Cooking Clubhouse on Yahoo was featuring a waffle/falafel/fajita last week), has encouraged a new category of multicultural cocktails, or fusion drinking.

There are Caribbean cosmopolitans and Portuguese gimlets to be had right now, and every specialty menu worth its lemon-in-salt has cross-dressed a standard cocktail like the martini in a couple of national costumes.

At Tabla, the restaurateur Danny Meyer's fusion Indian restaurant on Madison Square Park, the house drinks are inspired by India. You don't find Angostura bitters or Tom Collins mix in these cocktails. You find cinnamon sticks and cumin seeds.

The martini, or the Tablatini, is a fruit soup with vodka, basically, by its creator's own confession.

"I'm a big fan of fruit soups," said Floyd Cardoz, the executive chef and an owner at Tabla, who was born in Bombay and who had a pineapple-and-lemongrass soup, much like the Tablatini, on his menu. "We were serving it one day, and doing cocktail testing in the back of the kitchen, and I thought, this might be good as a martini. When I was growing up, there was lemongrass in the yard. I like that citrusy nose."

Fruit soup isn't my idea of a great time, but Mr. Cardoz's cocktail is a consummate diplomat—well mannered, gently persuasive, suave on several levels. It has a low alcohol content, qualifying it as a punch that could be drunk with spicy food, too.

"Because it goes down very easily, you'd get people very drunk if it had a full measure of vodka," Mr. Cardoz explained.

What you want if you're making fusion cocktails at home is a designated bartender, as much as a designated driver, or you could be faced with a round of Moroccan martinis. I preferred Tabla's lime drop, a gin and lime with peeled, chopped ginger in it, which adds a nice tasty burn to the drink's sweetness and sourness. Mr. Cardoz said it was an homage to his father, who would drink a gin with lime every Saturday.

Mr. Cardoz has an unseen ace in his hand: a martini with Indian kokum juice, which is similar to tamarind, but he can't get it here. He's trying.

"I haven't had a miss yet," he said of his specialty cocktails.

Neither had I, until that night in Marrakesh.

TABLATINI

ADAPTED FROM TABLA

2 cups pineapple juice
8 stalks fresh lemongrass, 6 coarsely chopped
and 2 halved crosswise
4 small fresh pineapple wedges
8 ounces Absolut Citron vodka
Juice of 1 lime

In medium saucepan, simmer the pineapple juice with the chopped lemongrass for 15 minutes; let cool. Strain into a jar and chill. Spear the pineapple wedges with the halved lemongrass stalks.

To a pitcher with ice, add pineapple juice, vodka and lime juice. Mix and strain into 4 chilled martini glasses. Add the pineapple-wedge garnish.

Yield: 4 servings

ATOMIC WEAPON TESTING

Singapore Sling

In March 2003, U.S. troops entered Iraq.

HEY SAILOR.

There's serious drinking and there's not serious drinking, and the Singapore sling is definitely No. 2. Sitting beneath the blowfish lamps at Otto's Shrunken Head Tiki Bar and Lounge on East 14th Street, knees bumping split bamboo, how could you think otherwise? Martini experts, go suck an olive.

On Wednesday evening, Otto's was as deserted as an atoll. The bartender talked to a patron about copyrighting photographs.

"A photograph's a photograph, right?" she said. A woman being stood up played Nina Simone on the jukebox until people started arriving and the tunes turned to memory-lane alternative music like the Dead Kennedys—practically singalong for the early-thirties crowd.

Time for fun.

Otto's bills the Singapore sling as a "South Seas favorite" that is "lite and refreshing." The drink is basically gin and cherry brandy, like a version of Coke that Atlanta executives never got up the nerve to bottle. It is lite indeed—so soda-like that it tastes underage. You get carded two drinks later, when the gin hits and the brandy starts to hula.

The cocktail, invented in 1915 by Ngiam Tong Boon, a bartender at Raffles Hotel in Singapore, as legend reports it, has more variations than a lineup in a brothel. Pineapple, triple sec—you like it, it's yours. Raffles, though it serves what it calls the original, also says it lost Mr. Tong Boon's recipe years ago.

Steve Pang, an owner of Otto's, presents an honest Singapore sling, as simple and true to form as a sarong. The parasol and grass-skirt sipping straw are a concession to the drink's association with the Polynesian cocktail craze of the 1940s and 1950s, which produced the mai tai, a Trader Vic's specialty, and the zombie. It cannot be coincidental that an era that watched a Pacific theater of war, revisited by atomic weapon testing, thought to comfort itself with nostalgia for things native, creating island cocktails.

At Otto's, Singapore slings are selling. The house punch, Pang's Punch, is popular. In a world being shaken and stirred, drinking is a little less concerned with its own sophistications. The subject is, for now, not academic.

On Wednesday night, a small friendly room with a jukebox, not a television set, decorated as if it were in the middle of the ocean and not the desert, with the kind of silly-cocktails costuming that could have entertained even troops, seemed exactly the place to be in April 2003.

SINGAPORE SLING

ADAPTED FROM OTTO'S SHRUNKEN HEAD TIKI BAR AND LOUNGE

1 1/2 ounces gin
1 1/2 ounces cherry brandy
Sour mix
Soda
Fresh lime juice
Maraschino cherry and orange slice

Fill a pint glass with ice. Add the liquors. Fill nearly to the brim with sour mix. Add two splashes of soda plus a dash of lime juice. Pour in a shaker and shake to chill. Return to the glass and garnish with the cherry and orange.

Yield: 1 serving

YAM SENG

Blood-Orange Cabernet Martini & Coconut Cosmo

KUMMI KIM SAYS SHE THINKS A LOT and drinks a lot, so that would make her a thoughtful bartender. Ms. Kim, twenty-five, is also part of a vanguard in New York that is reinventing the vocabulary of cocktail making.

Asian restaurants, with the help of people like Ms. Kim, who is Korean, are creating Asian cocktails as specialty drinks that showcase the house style, starting at the bar. The popularity of Asian accents in international cooking is cracking open cocktail menus, too.

Ms. Kim, who works at Sumile, a new restaurant on West 13th Street with a Japanese fusion theme, is as likely to reach for a shiso leaf as a maraschino cherry. She makes mojitos with shiso in addition to mint. Shiso, or perilla, is a relative of mint and basil. Ms. Kim's mojito is more herbal, less sweet and entirely smart. It's a cooler that has graduated to a cocktail. She puts coconut in her cosmos and ginger in her martinis—the Pacific Rim, right on the edge of your glass.

Other new restaurants like Matsuri, Tadashi Ono's sushi commissary underneath the Maritime Hotel in Chelsea, and Temple, a Korean restaurant in the East Village, are serving pickled lemons and calamansi limes, mangosteen puree, soursop and yuzu fruits—

a Southeastern Asian local market at the bar. And they are mixing them with sake or shochu, a Japanese sweet-potato spirit, as readily as vodka or gin. The Biltmore Room, on Eighth Avenue between 24th and 25th Streets, makes a muddled cucumber drink with melon-infused sake that is a kind of British Hong Kong version of a Pimm's Cup.

At Bôi, a Vietnamese restaurant on East 44th Street, the house serves a rambutini, which features rambutan, a bright red fruit with tubercles that is indigenous to the Malay Archipelago; it looks like a spitball on a bad hair day.

"Yam seng!"—cheers to you!—as they shout in Chinese at bars and weddings in Kuala Lumpur.

On Monday evening at Sumile, Ms. Kim was demonstrating, in her immensely friendly but professionally watchful way, the finer points of what she is trying to do. She prefers Stoli Oranj vodka to Absolut Mandarin for her Blood-Orange Cabernet Martini, because she believes it is softer and less alcoholic smelling (and more appropriate to her drink), a fact she proved with two snifters and a splash of each.

Ms. Kim previously worked at Michael Jordan's, the steak house in Grand Central Terminal, and she seems to appreciate the standard bar and a hard night out. But she knows that she wants a Cabernet-Merlot blend for her red wine martini, because of its specific notes of spice. And she achieves it: the cocktail is seasoned as surely, and subtly, as if she had pinched powders into it.

A sniff and a sip produced a taste like a trail of incense, and that could be a worldly new direction in drinking.

BLOOD-ORANGE CABERNET MARTINI

ADAPTED FROM SUMILE

1 ounce blood-orange puree
1 ounce Stoli Oranj vodka
2 ounces Cabernet-Merlot
$1/_2$ ounce simple syrup
Edible flower

Shake the liquid ingredients with ice and strain into a chilled martini glass. Garnish with a flower.

Yield: 1 serving

COCONUT COSMO

ADAPTED FROM SUMILE

$1^1/_2$ ounces Olifant citrus vodka
$1/_2$ ounce Malibu rum
$1/_2$ ounce triple sec
$1/_2$ ounce fresh lime juice
$1/_2$ ounce Coco Lopez
Splash of white cranberry juice

Shake all the ingredients with ice. Strain into a chilled martini glass.

Yield: 1 serving

THE BIRTH OF A STAR

Kumquat Sour, Bo Hai & Kumquat Mojito

WHAT IS IT WITH THE KUMQUATS?

Several restaurants and bars currently have them on their cocktail menus, as specialty items in specialty drinks, including Shun Lee Palace on East 55th Street (kumquat with whiskey), Tabla on Madison Square Park (a kumquat mojito) and Riingo on East 45th Street, Marcus Samuelsson's new restaurant, which features a kumquat sour.

The kumquat, a fruit which looks like a Mini Me orange, is native to China, and historically, a bit of a connoisseur's pet—grown in pots as an ornament—because it's, well, kind of cute.

Kumquats are now grown commercially in California, Texas and Florida. Dade City has an annual kumquat festival in January. They can be eaten whole. The rind is sweet, with an acidic under-rind. The flesh, which can be sour, is frequently discarded.

As an element in a cocktail, kumquats take the predictable presence of citrus and make it unusual.

"I never thought a kumquat would work, but I love it," said Robert Kingsland, the general manager at Riingo, who developed the cocktails with Mr. Samuelsson, an owner, and Christian Post, who worked with Mr. Samuelsson at Aquavit, where Mr. Samuelsson made his reputation. "It's refreshing—a sweet taste but also very crisp and clean."

The kumquat sour, which also has a strong taste of fresh spice, is based on an infusion of kumquat in shochu, a Japanese spirit.

"The concept of the menu is American Japanese, like the food," Mr. Kingsland explained. "Take American cocktails, and their components, like 'sour,' and add Asian Japanese flavors to them."

This is not as simple as it sounds.

"There's a lot of trial and error," Mr. Kingsland said, then added, in a voice troubled by the rising recall of drinks tested and best left undiscovered, "There's a lot of trial and error."

A coconut-infused rum, which was the centerpiece of a chocolate cream dessert cocktail, tasted superb, but "when you mixed the drink, it looked like a curdled custard, with a sheen," he said. "The coconut oil just rose to the top. It was disgusting."

The kumquat sour suffers no flaws. The color, its strength beyond its recipe, is astonishing—a pale silk-pajama yellow.

Nor does the Bo Hai, which is Riingo's martini. There are more cocktails out there claiming to be martinis at this point than cousins crowding a lawyer's office at the reading of a will, but the Bo Hai, which is gin and plum sake garnished with a sake-pickled plum, has a legitimate claim as an heir.

Dry, adult and unconcerned with immature palates, it is a martini. And it is different, too.

At Riingo on Monday evening, the bartender on duty looked like a young Coleen Dewhurst. Ms. Dewhurst complained to a patron about the lack of storage that Riingo's design ethic—a dramatically and darkly staged lounge with Asian overtones like arrangements of thick bamboo stalks—afforded her personal possessions.

"There's nowhere to put anything," she said, then lowered her face to his as though she were going to tell him, in a tight closeup, where the bodies were buried.

"Presentation is the key, my friend."

In the draped shadows of the window seating, an older Caucasian man sat with a younger Asian man, talking over two cocktails in the low, unhurried tone of a transaction.

I had three revelations in rapid order: the Bo Hai is the new martini; plum sake is the new vermouth; and plums are the new olives. No, I hadn't been drinking. I was just getting started.

The Bo Hai is the birth of a star, a translation so true to the spirit of the original that you may find yourself preferring it occasionally for the poetry alone.

KUMQUAT SOUR

ADAPTED FROM RIINGO

3 ounces kumquat-infused shochu *(see Note)*
3 ounces fresh lemon or lime juice
Kumquat

Stir the shochu and lemon or lime juice with ice. Strain into a Collins glass filled with ice. Garnish with a kumquat, split and wedged onto the glass's rim.

Yield: 1 serving

Note: Infuse 1 liter of shochu (typically, a bottle) with 5 ounces dried kumquats, which are generally available in Asian markets. Let the kumquats steep for 3 weeks before straining the shochu for use.

BO HAI

ADAPTED FROM RIINGO

5 ounces Tanqueray No. Ten gin
3 ounces Hakusan plum sake
Umeboshi plum

Shake the gin and sake vigorously with ice. Strain into a chilled martini glass and garnish with the plum.

Yield: 1 serving

KUMQUAT MOJITO

ADAPTED FROM TABLA

4 to 5 kumquats, cut in half
Pinch of fresh mint plus 1 sprig
1 ounce simple syrup
3 ounces light rum
$^1/_2$ ounce fresh lime juice
Splash of soda water

Muddle the kumquats, mint and syrup in a glass. Fill with ice. Add rum and lime juice and top off with soda. Garnish with a mint sprig.

Yield: 1 serving

COURTLY EVEN IN ITS DISGUISES

Sake Sunrise

Remedy has come and gone, but interest in sake has only broadened. Decibel in the East Village, which caters to a punk-rock and sake-drinking crowd, is a good starting point for would-be connoisseurs.

I ASSOCIATE SAKE WITH TWO-HANDED SIPPING and head-bowing ceremony, not a harmonica-happy Stevie Wonder mix. But if you visit Remedy, a restaurant and lounge that opened last month in New York, you'll find sake is running hard with a different posse these days—the thirsty warlords of the drinks-and-dating scene, hands on hilts as they put their best muscle on getting past the door.

On Wednesday night, in the combat zone of nightclubs-with-dining on East 20th Street near Park Avenue South, Remedy was leaping like carp in a pond. There were men in fedoras and women in newsboy caps stacking the white-light bar, working their silver cell phones and stretching their expensive legs in the low seating. A crystal chandelier revolved overhead, like a twenty-first-century version of a disco ball. People paced the sidewalk outside the glass window-wall, strategizing their perp walk toward the multiracial Mod Squad at the reservations desk. A yellow Hummer sat parked in the street.

Yes, there is a Stevie Wonder revival going on, and Mr. Wonder's *Songs in the Key of Life* faded on Turntable A into more funk-hop from the 1970s on B, as people negotiated little puddles of funny-flavored sake in little ceramic cups and carafes.

Remedy sells a menu of custom-blended sakes, which are sakes infused with dried lemons and apples and rose petals and Asian teas and ginger and vanilla. They have names like Sake Sunrise. (There is a Sake Therapy Lounge downstairs at Remedy, open on weekends, where a blond woman in black stood introducing herself to five men seated on a banquette on Wednesday night. "I wrote the lyrics and the melody," she said, taking a breath. Good luck.)

The reality—Sake Sunrise, and the menu's other mood drinks, is a New Age wine cooler, a spa cocktail. But it's good, and it grows on you. You can feel it segue from weird liquor to nice, new taste like a smooth D.J. working two LPs.

Sake is a subtle drink. It is sometimes described as having *umami*, or criticized for its lack of *umami*. *Umami*, which some characterize as a flavor, like sweetness or sourness, is a quality of palatability and the degree to which something satisfies the palate. A Zen archer's version of "hitting the spot."

In the third century, sake was called *kuchikami no sake*, or "chewing in the mouth" sake. The village populace would chew rice or millet and spit it out into tubs to ferment.

Today, sake is brewed by fermenting steam-cooked rice with yeast. The quality depends on the rice and the water. Remedy has fifteen unblended sakes to try. There are more than ten thousand brands in Japan. California makes sake, too. Eighty percent of sake produced is *futsuu-shu*, or "normal sake," with added distilled alcohol. It is basically cheap house wine, which is why it is now traditionally served warmed. The other 20 percent, *tokutei meisho-shu*, or the six premium sake categories—*junmai dai-ginjo, dai-ginjo, junmai ginjo, ginjo, junmai* and *honjozo*—are rice and water only, and are served slightly chilled. Professional tasters in Japan taste sake at room temperature.

David Bakhash, Remedy's manager, a gracious man with a shaved head and a seven o'clock shadow, wearing a black leather jacket and a diamond pinky ring that spelled "DB," served Sake Sunrises to my table on Wednesday—the most improbable geisha imaginable.

But sake, courtly even in its disguises, might yet make princes of us all.

SAKE SUNRISE

ADAPTED FROM REMEDY LOUNGE
AND RESTAURANT

1 tablespoon dried apricot, chopped
1 tablespoon dried peach, chopped
$1/2$ teaspoon ginger, chopped
$1/4$ vanilla pod *(about 1 inch of the pod)*
1 liter room-temperature sake *(any sake)*
1 cup hot sake, just below boiling

Combine the dry ingredients in a closeable basket strainer. Immerse in hot sake and steep for 2 hours. Add the room-temperature sake and put in a cool place (40 to 55 degrees F). Infuse with the strainer in liquid for 1 week. Remove the strainer. Serve the sake chilled, shaken with ice. The sake will keep for 1 week, refrigerated.

Yield: 10 servings of 4 ounces each

WHERE THE SOUTHWEST MEETS THE FAR EAST

Kentucky Turban & Blenheim Rum Ginger Snap

THE BRIGHT FOOD SHOP, SITTING AS HUMBLY as a fire hydrant at the corner of 21st Street and Eighth Avenue in Chelsea, pretty much defines the notion of a neighborhood spot.

It is a diner that, since it was taken over by Stuart Tarabour and Dona Abramson, who are now husband and wife, in 1991, has had improbably good food—short order but stylish. Mr. Tarabour preceded it slightly, with Kitchen Market, an ethnic food store, which he opened in 1985.

Last summer, Bright Food Shop expanded its dining room and opened a small cocktail bar. Ms. Abramson, the executive chef, created a cocktail list consistent with her interests in food, which focus on Tex-Mexican, Latin American and Asian. Ms. Abramson's nickname in Boston, where she worked years ago at the Ritz-Carlton, then at a restaurant called Harvest, was "Salsa."

Bright's menu announces at the top that it is, in a regional truckstop kind of way, "Where the Southwest Meets the Far East." In place of hardbitten twice-divorced waitresses of a certain age, who can pour a cup of coffee backhanded, Bright has men in black T-shirts who could be employees at a yoga center.

The four-seat cocktail bar's counter has a 1950s boomerang Formica design and coffee shop sugar dispensers hang above it as do-it-yourself lighting fixtures. Three citrus-colored lighted votivos lend a little evening mood. It might almost be a bar at home, set up in a kitchen corner.

On a sparse Monday, at several tables, young professionals met for dinner, still dressed in the athletic shoes that got them to and from their offices, to discuss the more routine matters that make people friends. It was an off-night for the gay boulevarding on Eighth Avenue, which crowds it like a parade on weekends and in good weather.

"Good night, my dear," said a patron to a waiter, leaving after her meal, still clutching her plastic-bottled water from a day at work.

Bright's cocktails are largely based on ingredients that Ms. Abramson likes to cook with, or that Mr. Tarabour stocks next door at Kitchen Market.

"I'm really a food person," said Ms. Abramson, who has no previous experience inventing drinks. "Creating cocktails is like any other recipe—it's flavors and contrasts."

Ms. Abramson questioned whether she would be likely to order Bright's cocktails, if she hadn't come up with them.

"I mean, I drink," she said. "I'll have a vodka gimlet or a margarita. But I wouldn't order a concoction, like a Sex on the Beach."

The Blenheim Rum Ginger Snap, a rum and lime juice drink, features Blenheim ginger ale, a soda with an intense ginger "heat" produced in South Carolina, which is a bit of a cult item. Celebrities like Penn Jillette, the magician, have wrapped their famous hands around the bottle.

The Ginger Snap, on ice in a soda glass, runs hot and cold on the palate. It's a fusion Southside—a limeade with a curry-like kick.

There is also a Tibet Libre and a Purple Corn Daiquiri, which is beautiful, but too mysterious for my taste. It might grow on you. In Latin America, people eat corn fungus, too.

Ms. Abramson's pride and joy is the Kentucky Turban. It is bourbon and chai, the Indian spice milk tea, with coconut milk as a creamer.

"It sounds really weird, but it's been selling well," she said. "I wanted to do a drink with chai. I thought, 'It's got to go with something.' Bourbon. It smells earthy and woody. I had a fun summer developing that cocktail."

When Kitchen Market, then Bright Food Shop, opened in Chelsea, the neighborhood was not the intersection of nightlife that it is now.

Ms. Abramson recalled, "We used to joke that if all the regulars came in one night, we'd be empty the next night."

As a grace note, the restaurant serves a fortune cookie on a plate with the diner's check.

On Monday, after a cocktail on a quiet night, my cookie read, "You are a person of culture."

KENTUCKY TURBAN

ADAPTED FROM BRIGHT FOOD SHOP

1 ounce bourbon
2 ounces Tazo organic chai concentrate
2 ounces "lite" coconut milk *(see Note)*
Orange slice

Fill a highball glass with ice. Pour in the bourbon, chai and coconut milk. Garnish with an orange slice.

Yield: 1 serving

Note: "Lite" coconut milk will mix better than full, Ms. Abramson explained.

BLENHEIM RUM GINGER SNAP

ADAPTED FROM BRIGHT FOOD SHOP

1 ounce rum
4 ounces Blenheim ginger ale *(see Note)*
Candied ginger slice
Lime wedge

Fill a highball glass with ice. Add rum and fill to the top with ginger ale. Garnish with a ginger slice and lime wedge.

Yield: 1 serving

Note: Bright Food Shop uses "gold cap" "not so hot" Blenheim ginger ale. Ms. Abramson explained that the red cap "hot" or the diet would work equally well, depending on how much spice one wants in one's drink.

BUGS FOR LUNCH

Tamarind Rum Punch

IS THE DALAI LAMA THE NEXT TRADER VIC?
Spice Market, Gray Kunz and Jean-Georges Vongerichten's restaurant and lounge on 13th Street at Ninth Avenue, makes a strong case for it. In the Polynesian palaces of yore, baby boomers instructed in the art by their parents cut loose with their looniest doings, high on mai tais.

Spice Market is movie Tibet—big-lot Buddhism. The two-level, 13,000-square-foot space provides an Indiana Jones–style sound stage for the new globalism. The restaurant, with a menu developed from the foods of Vietnam, Indonesia, India, Malaysia, Burma and Thailand, is itself ethnically mixed, or "globally brown."

On Wednesday night, designer fragrances perfumed the air like incense. Packed to its imported worm-eaten raw-wood rafters, Spice Market reminded me of the banquet scene in *The Temple of Doom,* when Willie Scott, Indy's blond nightclub singer sidekick, declines a platter of insects by saying, "No thanks, I had bugs for lunch."

The restaurant, designed by Jacques Garcia with Mr. Vongerichten, and the staff, dressed in saffron-orange by Alpana

Bawa, a Punjabi designer based in New York, look digitally enhanced. Spice Market is the DVD edition of a theme restaurant.

The crowd was a crowd, seen watering everywhere at the city's lounges, genetically engineered by the world awarenesses of the Internet, wireless devices and cocktail culture.

This is a group that can get three olives off a skewer resting in a martini glass with the adroitness that their parents showed with a roach clip or rolling papers. They no longer need to buy or read *Wallpaper* magazine. They were born, as adults, under its sign.

At the bar, a woman in leather pants said, "I'm wearing leather pants," as she settled on a stool and pulled the bar nuts—wasabi peanuts and Chinese five-spice almonds—to her elbow. She ordered a vodka martini, "but dirty," she explained to the bartender. Her companion chose a house special, a blood-orange mojito, discussing mojitos and blood oranges knowledgeably, as though they were rum and Cokes. The woman in the leather pants began a story about being a house guest somewhere.

"There was no reception in the place," she complained, speaking of the cell phone service.

Spice Market's cocktail menu includes a mai tai, the drink invented in 1944 by Victor "Trader Vic" Bergeron at his restaurant in Oakland, California. But the rum cocktail that is more to the point is rum tamarind punch, a Spice Market original, which extends the tradition of exotic punches popularized by Trader Vic's international franchise in the 1950s with pedigree and surprise. It is two ingredients, aged rum and tamarind nectar, a juice beverage, and it is sensational.

Sweetly spiced and lightly spirited, it was conceived to be compatible with a meal, said Chuck Simeone, the beverage director.

In my opinion, it would wash down even bugs.

TAMARIND RUM PUNCH

ADAPTED FROM SPICE MARKET

1½ ounces Ron Zacapa Centenario
2½ ounces tamarind nectar

Fill a bartender's glass with ice and add the ingredients. Shake and strain into a highball glass two-thirds full of fresh ice.

Yield: 1 serving

STRONG WATER

GIN EITHER MAKES YOU CRY OR FIGHT

The Bombardier

The Judson Grill closed in July 2004.

THE DIRTY LITTLE SECRET OF THE MARTINI CRAZE, said James Stuart, twenty-eight, a bartender at Judson Grill in Midtown Manhattan and the singer in Rearview, a rock band, is that most people today think they are going to get vodka when they order it and not gin, the martini's actual birthright.

And that makes Mr. Stuart, who is a gin drinker, who is English, whose parents are pub owners and who said he "grew up in the business" of drinking, as sad as a ballad sung tightly into a rasping microphone.

"People have a bad association with gin," said Mr. Stuart, who is out to change all that.

Gin was called "strong water" in England in the eighteenth century, at the height of the "gin craze."

"I once heard someone tell me that gin either makes you cry or fight," Mr. Stuart added. "I've personally never let it get to that point."

At the invitation of the restaurant's chef, Mr. Stuart, a spike-haired blond man built like a rugby player, who has worked at Judson Grill for six years, invented the Bombardier several weeks ago, a gin drink for the bar's summer cocktail menu.

"Being a bit of a purist, I didn't really relish the idea of coming up with a new cocktail in 2002," he said. "Modern cocktails can be offensive." Mr. Stuart drinks gin and tonics, with a "liberal dash of bitters," he said. He is also a "big negroni drinker—Campari, gin, sweet vermouth. That's a beautiful summer cocktail."

He explained, "I wanted to challenge myself to come up with something accessible that would also respect gin."

The Bombardier mixes gin with fresh citrus—both orange juice and lime—and is garnished with fresh mint.

"Gin sort of has an aromatic floral edge to it, and they complement that nicely," Mr. Stuart said. "The secret, I would say—and the surprise—is the touch of grenadine, which mellows the gin and makes it palatable to a gin novice." Tonic water and club soda in tandem give the Bombardier a light sparkle.

Mr. Stuart uses classic Bombay gin, not the fashionable Sapphire label making a determined round of marketing appearances at parties in New York recently.

Is the drink a cheat to a determined gin drinker? Too friendly by half with its pool raft of seasonal flavors?

"You can't get too preachy," said Mr. Stuart, who noted that the drink is having success at his bar, at times at his prompting with the gin-timid. It also has a money-back guarantee. "It's part of my plan to open people's palates—and minds—to gin. It's one of the great forgotten liquors."

Gin's true beauty, Mr. Stuart said, is its initial inaccessibility—like any of the world's great truths.

"It's an acquired taste," he said. "For those of us who honor the cocktail, the best things require an apprenticeship."

For the record, Mr. Stuart is a Guinness drinker, too.

THE BOMBARDIER

ADAPTED FROM JUDSON GRILL

2 ounces Bombay gin
$1/4$ ounce orange juice
$1/2$ ounce fresh lime juice
3 ounces club soda
3 ounces tonic
Dash of Grenadine
Fresh mint leaf

Shake the liquid ingredients in a shaker and pour into a highball glass over ice. Float the mint leaf.

Yield: 1 serving

THE ORAL TRADITION, NICELY ICED

The Martini

THE MARTINI DOESN'T NEED ME. It is the world's most famous cocktail, and likely to remain so. But it's lucky to have people like Dale DeGroff and John Conti.

Mr. DeGroff is a celebrity bartender and an authority on mixology, the self-styled "King of Cocktails," Lord of the Ring-a-ding-ding. He looks a little like George Clooney, and calls his wife "baby."

Mr. DeGroff is teaching a "cocktail college" at the Marriott Marquis on Broadway, one class a month on categories of drinks. Last month's class, the first, was on the martini. I called Mr. DeGroff and asked him if he had had a star pupil and he said "yes" without hesitation.

It was John Conti. Mr. Conti sat front and center and took notes.

Last Sunday I drove to Pawling, New York, where Mr. Conti lives with his wife, Ann, and two teenage children, to meet him and to have him make me a martini. Mr. Conti, a postal worker, was set up in his kitchen at the counter, where he pours. His wife and children were at church.

Mr. Conti embodies the interest in cocktails. I was reminded of Ray Bradbury's novel *Fahrenheit 451,* set in a future in which books are banned and burned. People memorize books, word for word, to save them. If there is ever another Prohibition, Mr. Conti will be walking around with a perfect martini inside him. The oral tradition, nicely iced.

"You got it," Mr. Conti said, taking position, when I asked him to make me a martini. He had also incongruously, but kindly, set out bialys and butter for breakfast.

The two questions to answer about the martini are the ratio of gin to vermouth, and how to mix it—to shake or stir. Mr. Conti uses a 6 to 1 measure and stirs.

"If you like it drier, you need it drier," he said, as if it were an adjustment to medication. Mr. Conti uses a regular premium gin, like Boodles or Tanqueray, not one of the super-premiums like Ten or Wet, which he considers too aromatic for the drink.

Mr. Conti put ice and water into a martini glass to chill it.

"The glass has got to be ice cold, but not the freezer," he said, nodding toward his refrigerator. "It picks up odors, and ice freezes on the glass, too, like snow."

Mr. Conti put ice into a bartender's glass and poured his measures over it. He rested the glass on a bar towel so that it would not slip as he stirred. Mr. Conti stirred with a long-necked spoon, bent slightly so that it would follow the sides of the glass, a trick he learned from Mr. DeGroff.

"You slide the spoon down and twirl, as opposed to agitating," he said. "The whole idea of a martini is a smooth drink. Agitation introduces air." Mr. Conti added, "People say you bruise the liquor. I don't believe that—but it is a different texture."

Mr. Conti emptied the martini glass, and strained his cocktail into it in a circular motion, pouring on the sides of the glass, so that the liquid wouldn't splash, then dropped a pitted green olive into it.

For a "dirty" martini, Mr. Conti recommended adding a splash of olive brine to the drink, as a garnish, rather than adding it to the ingredients to be stirred.

Unlike the super-size 10-ounce cocktails popular now in bars and lounges, Mr. Conti serves a 4- to 5-ounce drink in a 7-ounce glass, "so it doesn't get warm before you finish it, and so you don't drink too fast or too much," he said.

"Why not have one of these, and you buy the next round, and it gives an opportunity for socializing," he said. "It also keeps your drink fresh. And it gives you a margin so you can walk around without spilling it."

How to drink the cocktail? Aside from, with pleasure?

"Hold the glass by the stem, and don't touch the bowl, or the drink will get warm," Mr. Conti said.

The martini was excellent. Mr. Conti, who appeared to get as much pleasure from making it as I got from tasting it, reached across the drink and shook my hand, beaming.

"When you're at the bar, you're connecting," he said. "The guy says, 'Well, how would you like it?' And you watch, and he's making yours for you, to really enjoy. It's all part of the joy of it.

"When people go to a bar, they're happy—and it's good to be a part of some happiness."

I agree. Cheers.

THE MARTINI

ADAPTED FROM JOHN CONTI

3 ounces gin
$1/_2$ ounce dry vermouth
Green olive

Chill a 7-ounce martini glass by filling it with the ice and water. Fill a professional bartender's glass, or a tall 16-ounce glass, two-thirds full with ice. Add gin and vermouth to the bartender's glass and stir with a long-necked spoon, keeping the spoon close to the side of the glass as you swirl the ice. Stir until the glass frosts, about 20 seconds. Empty the martini glass and strain the contents of the bartender's glass into it. Garnish with the olive.

Yield: 1 serving

A WILD CARD

Blue Moon

CLAY TOMPKINS IS MY OLDEST FRIEND, and Karen Moody Tompkins, since marrying him twenty years ago, is one of my oldest friends, too.

I watched them married at St. Michael's Episcopal Church on West 99th Street, one of two witnesses, after they eloped. Karen met Jeffrey Gill, the rector who agreed to marry them, at a cocktail party. The Tompkinses had their reception a few days before the wedding, while they waited twenty-four hours for their marriage request to clear at City Hall.

The Tompkinses live, with their daughters Frederica, seventeen, and Suzanne, fifteen, on the Upper East Side. Clay had something of an impressive résumé as a bachelor in the 1970s, and then married and made good on the adage that to accomplished and unrepentant womanizers will be sent daughters, to throw a fearful shadow on their attitudes toward libertinage.

I joined the Tompkinses last night at David Burke and Donatella, a new restaurant on East 61st Street, to try the cocktail menu. Mr. Burke made his reputation at the Park Avenue Cafe and Donatella Arpaia owns Bellini.

The restaurant, built into the ground floor of a townhouse and designed by Matthew Sudock of M Design, looks like an exotic and opulent home in a movie from the 1940s—a white-top bar, white upholstered bar stools, red leather club chairs, brass hanging lamps, Chinese-motif latticework, a white lacquered reception desk and framed contemporary art hung against mirrored walls. There are nods to decorative designers from that era, like Samuel Marx and James Mont, names that the auction houses and modernist galleries sell as "Hollywood High Style."

There is a funereal whiff of camp, too—like something starring Joan Crawford or directed by Douglas Sirk. Like many restaurants on the Upper East Side, David Burke and Donatella is expertly lighted to vivify the stage realities of elective surgery, off-season suntans and budget-less boutique clothes buying. There are more nips and tucks in the clientele than the upholstery.

Last night, lawyers and local titans and their wives crowded the entrance and bar, drinking red wine and Johnnie Walker Black and martinis with a twist. By all appearances, the restaurant is enjoying success.

But, forgive my preoccupation with cocktails, the specialty drink program is chaotic at best and cynical at worst.

The bar manager, Raafet Olian, in an inexplicable break from character, dismissed most of the drinks on the menu as having been hastily tested and uninteresting. The list's creator, Ged Martin, previously at Payard on Lexington Avenue, has departed David Burke and Donatella, a scant five weeks into its run. Ms. Arpaia, in a telephone conversation, called him talented but "volatile."

The house drink, the Belladonna, which was named for Ms. Arpaia, was unavailable because the kitchen had not sent out the ginger-orange puree required. And the Blue Moon, based on a fresh blueberry puree, which is another of the "chef's" touches meant to distinguish the cocktails, was being served with a commercial substitute and garnished with a raspberry.

Which is not to say that Mr. Olian, who was promoted when Mr. Martin left and whom Ms. Arpaia characterized as a "wild card," is unserious about his work. He is bartending aspiration itself. He studies at Barnes and Noble, reading cocktail books, but "I never copy," he explained. He invents drinks like the Vacation, which he produced on the spot for a patron at Bar Nine when he bartended there, because she said that she was exhausted and that she needed a vacation.

Karen Tompkins was Mr. Olian's latest cocktail muse. While her husband switched from Pinot Grigio to a Pinot Noir, Karen tasted a raspberry Flirtini that Mr. Olian set before her and asked her opinion of—a professional Valentine. She liked it.

Karen grew up in the 1950s in Tulsa, Oklahoma, a dry state at the time. Oklahoma Senate Bill No. 55, the "Bone-Dry Law," was repealed in 1959. Karen recalled the bootlegger's back door deliveries to her parents' house.

"His name was Earl," she said, sitting at Mr. Olian's bar, providing inspiration. "When the truck arrived, it dragged the ground. When it left, it was back up on its tires." Earl was the "society" bootlegger, Karen's mother and aunt told her, because of all of the town's bootleggers, only Earl dressed well and he had a nice truck. He would call ahead and ask clients to leave their garage doors open, to make the delivery discreet.

An "Oklahoma Bootlegger" wouldn't be a bad idea for a drink. I hope Mr. Olian was paying attention.

BLUE MOON

3 ounces Beefeater Wet gin
1 ounce blueberry puree *(see Note)*
Club soda
A few fresh blueberries

Combine the gin and blueberry puree in a cocktail shaker with ice. Shake until chilled and strain into a highball glass filled with ice. Top off with club soda. Garnish with blueberries.

Yield: 1 serving

Note: For blueberry puree, puree fresh blueberries with sugar in a blender, in a ratio of 2 tablespoons blueberries to $^1/_4$ teaspoon sugar. Strain through a chinois.

AN APERITIF IN BLACK TIE

The Tuxedo

PEACE ON EARTH TO ME IS A HOTEL BAR. Better yet, a lobby lounge that serves cocktails. It is an idea as metropolitan, in the best sense, as, well, cocktails.

"They're part of the civic fabric, like the New York Public Library or Central Park," said Thomas Connors, author of *Meet Me in the Bar,* an appreciation of American hotel bars.

New York has several great hotel bars and lounges, including the Cafe Pierre Bar in the Pierre Hotel, presided over most evenings by Richard Weyant; Fifty Seven Fifty Seven in the Four Seasons Hotel, where Jeffrey Garcia tends bar with sympathy and knowledge; the Bemelmans Bar at the Carlyle Hotel, where Luis Serrano works with patience and grace; and the King Cole Bar at the St. Regis Hotel, where one finds a gentleman named Gavin Fitzgibbon.

The Mandarin Oriental, New York, which opened in November at 80 Columbus Circle, has done right by me. On the thirty-fifth floor, beyond the lobby, is the Lobby Lounge—a warm well of comfortable seating and flattering light with a King Kong–size conversational view of Central Park and the city.

Experience and well-trained reserve used to be what you paid for in a hotel bar or lounge. And you pay. More typically today it is a weird servitude, of which the Mandarin Oriental is an example.

On Wednesday night, the servitude pulled thin when the staff overstressed during the holiday crush. Rain streaked the lounge's windows like the sorrows of the world and the hotel reception's grand circle of ceiling lights, reflected in the glass, hung out over the cogs of traffic in Columbus Circle like a halo.

"I am in charge here," a woman seating guests said to a couple who tried to break rank and seat themselves after a confusing wait in a lengthening queue. We tightened our line like kindergartners dressed for the snow.

But things smoothed over when seated and served.

I requested a Tuxedo because requests are at the heart of a good bar. The Tuxedo is a gin martini–like cocktail spiced with anise, which was popular in the nineteenth century and reappeared during Prohibition in a variation that called for sherry instead of anise liqueur. It is sometimes called a turf cocktail and is similar in ingredients to an income tax.

Ask a bartender unfamiliar with the Tuxedo to go lightly on the anise, usually a pastis like Pernod, which is overpowering to the drink. Properly proportioned, it is an aperitif in black tie—convivial and dressed to kill. (A white tie is Benedictine, bourbon and vodka; a top hat is apricot brandy, vermouth, vodka and Cointreau.)

As I looked out the window and into the lobby, the Mandarin Oriental, with its silver Chinese cloud motif, began to remind me of the mythical lamasery in Frank Capra's 1937 *Lost Horizon*. (Mr. Capra claimed the Christmas season with another classic, *It's a Wonderful Life*.)

A group of air travelers who crash in the Tibetan mountains are rescued and taken to Shangri-La, a city beyond the storm where the world outside, braced for war in 1937, is a fiction and the peace within is a dream come suspiciously true.

Hotel lobbies give you that kind of room to think.

THE TUXEDO

ADAPTED FROM THE MANDARIN ORIENTAL, NEW YORK

1 ounce gin
1 ounce dry vermouth
2 dashes of Pernod
2 dashes of maraschino liqueur
2 dashes of orange bitters
Maraschino cherry

Stir the ingredients with ice and strain into a chilled cocktail glass. Garnish with a maraschino cherry.

Yield: 1 serving

THE TODDY EFFECT

Juniper and Berries & Hot Buttered Cider

IF ANYBODY COULD ASK THE CITY TO TURN the temperature down so that he could serve a warm cocktail, it might be
Daniel Boulud, the French restaurateur who has become something
of a force of nature himself in New York since arriving in 1982.

Mr. Boulud's winter cocktail menu, introduced on Monday at his
signature restaurant, Daniel, on East 65th Street, includes Juniper
and Berries, a warm apple-cider-like drink with gin, crème de cassis and maple syrup. (Coincidentally, the Clinton Bakery on the
Lower East Side is also serving a warm apple and maple drink, without liquor. Throw some gin into it, guys!)

When the temperature takes an icy dive, my brain puts in a non-
negotiable request for the toddy effect. I basically want to mull my
body with heated spirits.

Daniel's winter cocktails, which were developed by Francesco
Lafranconi, a bartender in Las Vegas, were unveiled at a party on
January 12. It was reassurance of a kind that Mr. Boulud's elegant
lounge and bar, inside and to the right of the revolving-door
entrance with its discreet opaque glass, can get as lively as Live
Bait, a loud and rowdy student union of a restaurant and bar on

East 23rd Street. People stacked up three deep to get Mr. Lafranconi's attention, and the elbows were out—they were just really richly covered elbows.

On Wednesday, the night after a big snow, things were slower. Daniel's lounge-bar has the look of the interior of an executive jet—waxed wood paneling, real art, plush velvet seating.

The bar is gold-topped and has a black-and-white piano-key edge. Behind it, an arrangement of white amaryllis rose toward the coffered ceiling like a pipe organ. There were a lot of neatly suited employees milling around without much to do, and the general hush, reinforced by the low light of the pleated-silk lampshades, felt like a casino off-season—Monte Carlo in March.

A table of young Americans and Europeans discussed money in various accents. French movie jazz played in the background. At the bar alone, a woman in a black sleeveless cocktail dress sipped a glass of wine while reading a book. Was her name Amélie? Central casting!

I nursed my haute toddy and ate tiny olives. The Juniper and Berries is a true recipe: an inevitable blend of its ingredients. You taste everything, the lemon, the clove, and yet nothing but the cocktail itself. Savory and sweet, it has the good cook's sense of a traditional winter dish. Game with cherries, or bollito misto and mostarda. There's nothing wrong with the heat at Daniel, but the drink is also pleasantly warm—*tiède,* in the vocabulary of presentation of French restaurants.

Half a cocktail later, you might find yourself praying for snow.

JUNIPER AND BERRIES

ADAPTED FROM DANIEL

1 ounce gin
1 ounce crème de cassis
2 ounces apple juice
$3/4$ ounce fresh lemon juice
1 tablespoon maple syrup
Lemon zest and 3 cloves
Fresh red currants

Put the liquid ingredients in a saucepan. Add the lemon zest, pierced with the cloves. Warm for about 2 minutes over medium heat but do not boil. Strain. Serve in a tempered-glass mug. Garnish with currants.

Yield: 1 serving

HOT BUTTERED CIDER

ADAPTED FROM CLINTON BAKERY

8 ounces apple cider
2 pieces star anise
2 cloves
$1/2$ teaspoon ground cinammon
2 tablespoons maple butter
1 cinnamon stick

Heat the ingredients, except the cinammon stick, in a saucepan over low heat to melt the butter. Strain into a mug or heatproof glass. Garnish with a cinnamon stick

Yield: 1 serving

WORTH THE NOSEDIVE

Gin Blossom & Way of the Dragon

"SOMEONE'S WEARING WHITE DIAMONDS," said the Asian bodybuilder, with his tattoos crawling up his arms, on duty at the Biltmore Room bar.

Two very "done" ladies with tall delicate pastries of hair styling were unwrapping themselves at the door for the trip through the lounge back to the dining room.

I was at the bar drinking the Way of the Dragon. More about that later.

The Biltmore Room is a peculiar place on the map, in more ways than one. The cooking, devised by Gary Robins, the executive chef and a famous fusionist on the New York restaurant scene, is Asian inspired, though the menu visits the Maryland eastern shore, Italy and Morocco as well. The restaurant, in a space that was formerly a gay club called Rome, is on Eighth Avenue in a no-man's-land above 23rd Street. It retained the club's vault-like gold entrance gates and marble, which are in fact demolition bric-a-brac from the Biltmore Hotel near Grand Central Terminal.

Citizens of no-man's-land seem to patronize the Biltmore Room— a curious combination of neighborhood nobody-in-particulars and foodies there for Mr. Robins's excursion tours.

The lounge and bar area has a dull-bronzed ceiling, square crystal-shaded hanging lamps and a satin and velvet upholstered seating area with black cocktail tables that have moongate cutouts in them. It looks like the reception area of a very high-end Hong Kong escort service.

But the bartender was knowledgeable, about the drinks and the menu, and he runs a bar which is harmless and friendly, not vicious or snotty like bars with a harder, hotter scene.

And several drinks, which were created by Willie Shine, the beverage director, are worth the nosedive.

The Gin Blossom is a gin rickey of sorts, a tonic-spritzed highball based on gin that the Biltmore Room infuses in house with basil. In place of simple syrup, there is elderflower syrup.

A gin blossom, colloquially, is the red nose caused by capillaries and a skin condition called roseacea, commonly associated with drinking too much. The comedian W. C. Fields cultivated a gin blossom that was a garden-club show-stopper.

The Biltmore Room's Gin Blossom is an excellent cocktail. The taste of basil is strong and unexpected, and the elderflower cuts its herbal power with a touch of sweetness—a neat reverse on most cocktails, which use herbs to balance sugar instead.

The bartender's pride is the Way of the Dragon. It is one of the most exotic drinks I have tried, including a monsoon of new Asian cocktails, in a year of drinking dangerously.

"Not done yet," the bartender said when I started to sip the martini glass. He dusted the top of the cocktail with cayenne. "One last," he added, when I started to sip again, and he dropped a mint leaf in.

The drink is a mandarin-flavored vodka drink, with calamansi lime juice, honey and mint. The calamansi lime is a small, extremely sour lime, popular in the Philippines, that tastes like a lemon crossed with a mandarin orange.

The bartender shook the drink vigorously when making it, which produced a pale jade cocktail topped with a white-mink froth.

"Someone's wearing White Diamonds," he said, as two done ladies unwrapped at the door.

By all appearances, it could have been my cocktail.

GIN BLOSSOM

ADAPTED FROM THE BILTMORE ROOM

1 1/2 ounces basil-infused gin *(see Note)*
1/4 ounce elderflower syrup
Tonic water
Basil leaf

Shake the gin and elderflower syrup with ice and strain onto fresh ice in a Collins glass. Top off with tonic water and garnish with basil leaf.

Yield: 1 serving

Note: Infuse a 750 ml bottle of gin by mixing in a glass container with a small bunch of fresh basil. Let sit for 24 hours and strain back into the original bottle.

WAY OF THE DRAGON

ADAPTED FROM THE BILTMORE ROOM

2 1/2 ounces Hanger 1 Mandarin vodka
1 ounce calamansi lime juice
1/2 ounce sour mix
Dash of honey
Cayenne pepper
Pinch of mint, plus 1 leaf

Combine the ingredients, except the cayenne and mint leaf, in a bartender's glass with ice and shake until chilled. Strain into a martini glass and sprinkle the top of the cocktail lightly with cayenne. Garnish with a mint leaf.

Yield: 1 serving

A SERIOUS WORK TOOL

The Gimlet

I'M NOT NAMING NAMES, BUT I HAD THE WORST GIMLET of my life a few weeks ago in a restaurant in St. John's, Newfoundland. It came in an ugly martini glass to boot. It could have been my fault. I looked the bartender in the eye and asked her, when I ordered it, how she was going to make the drink. Maybe I spooked her. (Canada's most popular cocktail is the caesar: a bloody mary with Clamato juice. You be the judge.)

The gimlet is my favorite cocktail, and it is not a cocktail to be toyed with. Bartenders try. I have been served gimlets with Rose's Lime Juice (a lime syrup) and no fresh lime juice. I have been served gimlets with fresh lime and no Rose's.

I have been served (O Canada!) a gimlet with bottled lime juice and a tablespoon of sugar added, as though it were a recipe for pie. The experience was a sobering reminder (always ill timed as your cocktail is arriving) that only vigilance rewards when dealing with great ideas.

The gimlet's logic seems clear to me: gin or vodka, with Rose's Lime Juice and fresh lime juice in equal parts, shaken or stirred until ice cold and served straight up in a stemmed cocktail glass that is confident but not proud of its sex appeal. A standard martini glass with a light weight does nicely. The garnish—and a gimlet should have it (it's green water without one)—is a thin crescent moon of lime, floated in the drink invitingly, not perched on the side like a timid swimmer looking at a cold lake. Making a gimlet icy gives it smoothness when sipped.

"You have to have your liquor nice and chilled," said Jeffrey Garcia, a bartender at Fifty Seven Fifty Seven in the Four Seasons Hotel. "That's the best secret to it."

For that reason, it is an excellent summer drink. I have discovered that the gimlet is also an unexpectedly sophisticated fall-to-winter drink. Who wants to warm up, I realized, when you can have cool rational thoughts in temperate climates like the lobbies of good hotels: on career changes, relationship breakups and other personal accounting? The gimlet can be a serious work tool.

"It's a nice alternative to a martini," Mr. Garcia said. "It's a little lighter, for those who find a martini too strong. It has balance—not too sweet, not too overpowering."

Philip Marlowe, the detective, drinks gimlets on the job in Raymond Chandler novels. "A fellow taught me to like them," Marlowe tells a woman at a bar, who is drinking a gimlet, too, in *The Long Goodbye.*

The drink, by legend, was a gin drink invented late in the eighteenth century by sailors in the Royal Navy who received daily rations of gin and lime. The gimlet is a barrel-boring device that was sent with lime-juice casks to the British colonies.

I prefer vodka in the drink, for its understatement. Gin talks too much, with its juniper bush–berry accent. And what you want, as everyone knows, is a drinking companion who listens.

THE GIMLET

ADAPTED FROM FIFTY SEVEN FIFTY SEVEN BAR
AT THE FOUR SEASONS HOTEL

4 ounces vodka or gin
$^1/_2$ ounce fresh lime juice
$^1/_2$ ounce Rose's Lime Juice
Thin lime wedge

Combine the liquid ingredients in a cocktail shaker with ice. Shake and strain into a martini glass. Garnish with a lime wedge.

Yield: 1 serving

A BALLAD

Kind of Blue

AH, TO BE YOUNG(ISH), and worth a chunk of change, in New York.

Blue Smoke, a barbecue restaurant on East 28th Street, is one of the M.B.A. barns on the Park Avenue South strip, down the block from the Park Avenue Country Club and Houston's, across the avenue.

It is also Danny Meyer's take on a big beer-blast bar. Mr. Meyer is the celebrated restaurateur who created the Union Square Cafe, Gramercy Tavern, Eleven Madison Square and Tabla.

On Thursday night, Blue Smoke was crowded three deep with young(ish) money-makers drinking. If you've ever wondered who's moving into all those new luxury-rental buildings or driving the average price of a one-bedroom apartment past $500,000 in New York—and you're not one of them—you can drink with them at Blue Smoke.

The bar's televisions were tuned to ESPN, where a football player, in an interview, was dealing with his finer emotions. Aretha Franklin, Marvin Gaye and all the other artists who, historically, form the soundtrack of a bar scene in a college town or a home-game weekend fraternity party, played on Blue Smoke's sound system. (There is a live-jazz club downstairs, Jazz Standard, for the suaver at heart.)

But this is Manhattan, not the real deal.

A woman with a Vuitton bag drank beer from a bottle. Her companion, wearing his camel-cashmere topcoat, drank Guinness on draft. They were talking about dream real estate, which is what men and women discuss in mixed company today. If you're not in mixed company, you talk about men or women. A martini in a moisturized hand passed my ear periodically as the woman behind me retrieved and sipped and returned her glass to the bar as she went over a floor plan and prospectus with her companion.

I was an undergraduate in the 1970s at the real deal, the University of Virginia, whose student body prided itself on the fact that a *Playboy* magazine ranking of drinking schools had excluded the University of Virginia, refusing to list it because, as the article explained in a footnote, it didn't seem fair to include professionals in a survey of amateurs.

At UVa., Thursday only existed as a prelude to Friday—any bar would have pumped your chest with music and the drinking was calisthenic. You had twenty-four short hours before you had to do it seriously. There were a few too many A students at the bar at Blue Smoke.

The specialty cocktail list includes the Kind of Blue, which sells best downstairs at the jazz club, explained Malysa Volpicelli, the beverage director. It is named for the Miles Davis standard, and is a variation on the Aviation, a gin drink flavored with maraschino, an Italian cherry liqueur.

The Kind of Blue is based on Magellan gin, a French product, which arrived in the United States last summer and got noticed a lot because it's blue. It was developed by Michel Roux, the man behind the legendary Absolut vodka marketing. Mr. Roux worked on Bombay Sapphire, with its trademark blue bottle, and the feedback on that project was that people were disappointed to pour Sapphire and find that the gin itself wasn't an attractive blue.

Mr. Roux put himself on a mission to make a blue gin. Magellan is tinted through infusion with the purple flower of the iris root.

Blue sells. The cocktail market was welted with blue drinks several years ago, and blue is the appeal of recent cognac liqueurs like Hpnotiq and Envy, and blue curaçao. It goes well with club lighting and party-boat socials.

"You think of blue drinks, 'curaçao blue'—horrible," Ms. Volpicelli said.

The Kind of Blue is rescued by its jazz-cool pale blue and the taste of maraschino, which is distilled like brandy from marasca cherries and their pits, which are crushed and included and which give the liqueur, and the cocktail, an artisanal bitter-almond taste. In the nineteenth century, maraschino is what cherries were marinated in to produce "maraschino cherries," the drink garnish. Maraschino cherries are now brined chemically.

People drink to turn up the volume when they go out. A cocktail like the Kind of Blue turns it down. It is, at its best, a ballad. Played introspectively on a trumpet. Using a mute.

KIND OF BLUE

ADAPTED FROM BLUE SMOKE

2 ounces Magellan gin
$^1/_2$ ounce maraschino liqueur
1 ounce fresh lemon juice
Lemon twist

Pour the liquid ingredients into a bartender's glass filled with ice. Shake and strain into a martini glass. Garnish with a twist.

Yield: 1 serving

EVERYONE SNACKS THE OLIVE

The Gibson

LOOKS ARE EVERYTHING, AS ANY COCKTAIL DRINKER will tell you.

The right shaker, the right glass, the right garnish—you don't want anything less than perfect approaching your lips as you close your eyes for that first shy sip. Drink dirty well water with a ladle if you disagree.

Despite New Year's resolutions to be less superficial, I can't get past thin shakers, thick glasses or dumb garnishes. A cocktail should look as sharply executed as it tastes. Ounce for ounce, it is a precise measure of intention. You can relax when the drink's in your hand.

The simplest cocktails have the finest points. A gibson is a martini with an onion instead of an olive. So what? I can hear someone say.

Jacques Sorci, the executive chef for the Ritz-Carlton New York, Battery Park, buys small, sweet onions from an organic farm in Quakertown, Pennsylvania, and cooks and pickles them *à la grecque* in chicken stock, white wine vinegar, bay leaves and fresh thyme, to serve as a garnish for gibsons at Rise, the hotel's bar. That's so what.

The Rise gibson has an aesthetic singularity that commodifies its value as an experience like the pearl in an oyster.

"The martinis are twelve to fifteen dollars—you cannot justify the cost by just the view," Mr. Sorci said. Rise is on the fourteenth floor, overlooking New York harbor.

A black olive would make the gibson a buckeye. A niçoise olive would make it excellent, as my experience has shown.

Garnishes also produce slight infusions, the basic "twist" being the best example. Dale DeGroff, in *The Craft of the Cocktail,* devotes more than a page to the technique of the basic citrus twist. I had a knife taken away from me at a party I gave recently by a guest who lost patience with my preschool efforts to carve a piece of lemon for his cocktail. People care.

Rocking in the cool depths of designer vodkas, spa-moisturized by celebrity, the green martini olive, a legendary comeback like the drink itself, has become something of an industry force.

It lost the pimento like a college marriage and makes appearances in fancy food emporiums, hand-stuffed with chipotle peppers, blue cheese or garlic. It strikes marketing deals with the big vodka houses like Finlandia and Skyy, which package olives with liquor in promotions.

Saks Fifth Avenue, the department store, requested a private-label bar condiment program for its houseware boutiques last year, which included martini olives, maraschino cherries and gibson onions. The items were provided by Fodda, a New York specialty food company. Keith Bacon, its president, was previously in the fashion business, at Alfred Dunhill.

The Santa Barbara Olive Company, a twenty-year-old condiments company in California with twenty-five drink-related items, now has sales of more than $1 million a month, up 23 percent from 2001. The company is moving aggressively into mainstream supermarkets like Safeway and Piggly Wiggly, where awareness of the fashionability of cocktail accessories like olives is expanding most rapidly.

"Everyone 'snacks' the olive now," said Craig Maleka, who founded the company with his wife, Cindy, of the unusual olive stuffings. Jalapeño pepper is Mr. Maleka's big seller.

"The hot drink is the big thing," he said.

The Malekas had four competitors when they started. Based on exhibitors present at specialty food trade shows, Mr. Makela estimated that there are now five hundred companies vying for the pleasure of your garnish.

THE GIBSON

ADAPTED FROM THE RISE BAR AT THE
RITZ-CARLTON NEW YORK, BATTERY PARK

3 ounces gin
Touch of dry vermouth
Cocktail onions

Chill a martini glass. Fill a shaker with ice. Pour in the gin. Add the vermouth. Cover and shake. Put several cocktail onions on a stick and place in the chilled glass. Pour the cocktail over onions and serve.

Yield: 1 serving

TUMBLEWEEDING

Ten Sage

WE NOW ENTER THE CUTTHROAT WORLD of the corporate cocktail—not martinis at lunch, but the drinks created by committee at the headquarters of national restaurant chains like Restaurants Unlimited, in Seattle, where exciting trends are engineered, not born.

Take the case of the Ten Sage, which I ordered recently at Palomino in downtown Indianapolis.

The Ten Sage, which is gin with sage, lime sour and orange passion fruit liqueur, is a cocktail created in April by Don Adams, executive vice president for creative development at Restaurants Unlimited, and his colleagues.

It was the first cocktail in what Mr. Adams called a collection of "herbaceous" drinks, a line including thyme, basil, tarragon and rosemary cocktails that are featured in a separate section on a specialty-drink menu.

"This is one of the best spirit inventions that we've done," Mr. Adams said. "We're bringing the food element in. The public's very into that. The flavor profile is intense. The liquor companies have been way ahead of us, putting similar ingredients into their liquors.

If you take gin, and take the idea of juniper, and figure out what would go well with that—it's time to do that with cocktails."

Mr. Adams's company, with thirty restaurants coast to coast and a customer base of four million people, sells two million cocktails a year. New drinks are tested for four to six weeks in San Francisco and other cities, in groups of fifteen to twenty cocktails with a theme like herbs.

"We look at percentage of sales," Mr. Adams said. "A drink needs to get into the top 15 percent of cocktail sales within that period to be deemed a success." Success is Restaurant Unlimited's euphemism for survival. The ginger star caipirinha died hard in crowded bars.

Mr. Adams also takes research trips to cities like New York, to "start to look at what may be coming up in trends in cocktails," he explained.

Nationally, there are twelve Palominos, the company's "European influenced rotisserie restaurant/bar brand," according to Mr. Adams. Its clientele: people in feather-hued merino wool sweaters and beige gabardine suits making deals at midday. At what point did Middle American businessmen and -women start dressing like Hollywood agents?

At Palomino in Indianapolis, which is the brand's leader in annual sales, the restaurant is painted a chile red and looks like a supper club with Southwestern accents. A Fernand Léger–style cubist painting dominated the dining room. Jazz cocktail organ and guitar music played. Steely Dan came up next.

I ordered a Ten Sage with a wood-fired grilled hamburger on a toasted-garlic bun. The drink, with a sage leaf tumbleweeding lazily on the surface of the desert-pink liquid, was presented in a $7^1/_2$-ounce Cardinal Excalibur No. 3031428 martini glass, said Mr. Adams in Seattle. The drink was perfectly pleasant, which is its intention.

The Ten Sage is Mr. Adams's leading invention, setting the pace for sales now for the last seven months.

Not by chance, I was in good company. More than two hundred others ordered the cocktail that day.

TEN SAGE

ADAPTED FROM PALOMINO

1 1/2 ounces Tanqueray No. Ten gin
3 torn fresh sage leaves, plus 1 for garnish
1 1/2 ounces fresh lime sour
1/2 ounce Alizé Gold Passion

Pack a pint glass with ice and fill with all the ingredients. Shake well and serve strained into a 7 1/2-ounce martini glass. Garnish with a sage leaf.

Yield: 1 serving

TYPE B

Red Snapper

I'M NOT STUPID. It's the end of a three-day weekend, and the only cocktail you're going to be willing to read about, or mix, is a bloody mary.

The bloody mary would be an American classic—perfect as the last firework of a Fourth of July celebration—if it had been invented here. But it was invented at Harry's New York Bar in Paris in the 1920s, and arrived in New York with its inventor, Fernand Petiot, who was hired by Vincent Astor to work at his Fifth Avenue hotel, the St. Regis.

Petiot was also asked to rename the drink to appease delicate sensibilities. He called it the Red Snapper, which is how the hotel's King Cole Bar still presents it. The original Mary, depending on which wild goose you chase, was (1) Mary, Queen of Scots, who died in a bucket of blood; (2) Mary Tudor, who thirsted for Protestant blood; (3) a patron at the Bucket of Blood Club in Chicago; or (4) a woman who was repeatedly stood up at Mr. Petiot's bar in Paris, which is, as the English would say, pretty bloody.

The Red Snapper is a gin, not a vodka drink. An astute bartender will know that, though the St. Regis now serves its version with vodka.

But it is as the bloody mary, with vodka, that the cocktail became the country's house drink in the 1960s—a real workhorse, ready to start the day as a popular hangover remedy, show up at picnics and tail-gating parties, and the first to hit the patio as the sun dropped and the charcoal began to glow.

And there's the name, too, like a Nichols and May routine. Not just adult, but funny.

Vaguely nutritious because of the vegetable content, bloody marys were like multivitamins for WASPs. I had a college acquaintance at the University of Virginia in the 1970s, Bob Edens, the kind of frat boy who wore sunglasses indoors and played Monopoly with cash, who looked strangely unnatural without a bloody mary in his hand. Bob, wherever you are, cheers.

The bloody mary today is synonymous with the idea of brunch, and at brunch, everyone's a bartender with a secret—pickling seeds, wasabi powder, jalapeño peppers. Restaurants have introduced make-your-own bloody mary carts, more salad bar than bar. As a virgin mary or a bloody shame, the drink is apparently good without vodka. I wouldn't know.

I like the Red Snapper. It's a Type B bloody mary: basic, relaxed, assured. The St. Regis uses Sacramento tomato juice, which Gavin Fitzgibbon, tending bar on Tuesday, believes is the best.

Try one tonight. Or, tomorrow morning.

RED SNAPPER

ADAPTED FROM THE KING COLE BAR AT
THE ST. REGIS HOTEL

2 dashes of salt
2 dashes of black pepper
3 dashes of Worcestershire sauce
3 dashes of cayenne pepper
1 dash of lemon juice
1 ounce vodka
2 ounces tomato juice

Add the salt, peppers, Worcestershire sauce and lemon juice to a shaker. Add ice, vodka and tomato juice. Shake, pour into a highball glass and garnish if you wish.

Yield: 1 serving

SWEET

COCKTAIL NATION

White Hot Martini

On February 22, 2004, 10.6 million viewers watched HBO's comedy Sex and the City *draw to a close after six seasons on the air.*

A FEW NIGHTS AFTER THE FINALE OF *SEX AND THE CITY*, a television series that did as much to advance the popularity of cocktail drinking, especially among women, as a coordinated advertising campaign, I stopped into the Cutting Room, a lounge and music club on West 24th Street owned by Steve Walter and Chris Noth, *Sex*'s "Mr. Big."

The Cutting Room is Big's "struggling actor" or "college roomie" side—not a martini temple or a cigar bar but a now old-style lounge like the lounges that first appeared in the late 1980s and early 1990s when Generation X became legal and began drinking. There are velvet drapes on the windows and brass chandeliers with candle flame lightbulbs and it looks like someone's idea of someone's living room if their parents were away and had allowed them to have a party. Kurt Cobain, the suicide legend behind Nirvana, the band that defined Generation X with *Smells Like Teen Spirit* in 1991, would be thirty-four today if he had lived.

Technically, *Sex*'s Carrie Bradshaw and her cohorts were Gen Xers. Sarah Jessica Parker, who played Carrie, is thirty-six. And they all disappeared into commitment and engagement and marriage.

I was thinking about this as I watched the crowd at the Cutting Room. They were standing, talking in small groups, and balancing cocktail glasses. It was a workweek, weekday evening. These were the "average citizens" of the much-touted "cocktail nation"—catching up, touching base, keeping company. They were the college students who rediscovered big band and swing music in the 1980s and 1990s, music their grandparents, not their parents had grown up to, who were now nearing the edge of forty. It was like a mixer—a gentler venue for those who wanted to "be out" without the stress of "going out." As an acquaintance who is thirty-two put it, "I don't like going to a 'fight for your seat type place.'" Leave that to the young.

At the suggestion of a colleague, I tried the Cutting Room's White Hot Martini. The White Hot is a chocolate martini, despite the fact that it is as white as a washed poodle. It is a Gen X version of a Grasshopper, or other pastel "ladies' drinks" from the 1950s that include cream.

A cocktail is possibly the only place that you don't want to encounter chocolate, but the drink isn't bad. It's much better, in fact, than it deserves to be, given the candy-store ingredients. Chocolate cocktails have showed up on many specialty drink menus in the last five years, and one has to assume they're being ordered. Could it be that a martini glass could also be a grip on childhood, or is it a generational taste in drinking? Chocolate breakfast food in the evening.

I overheard a conversation once on a morning subway between two young men, hair falling into their faces but wearing suits.

"Yeah, it's in the back of the closet," one said to the other. He was talking about his skateboard.

As Mr. Cobain shouts hoarsely at the end of *Smells Like Teen Spirit*, "A denial, a denial, a denial."

WHITE HOT MARTINI

ADAPTED FROM THE CUTTING ROOM

$^1/_2$ ounce each Absolut Vanilia, Van Gogh Dutch
Chocolate Vodka, Godiva White Chocolate liqueur
$^1/_4$ ounce each Frangelico liqueur, butterscotch
schnapps, crème de cacao
Splash of Goldschlager liqueur
Freshly shaved white or dark chocolate

Shake the ingredients vigorously in a bartender's glass with ice.
Strain into a large chilled martini glass (at least 9 ounces). Garnish
with shaved chocolate.

Yield: 1 serving

BREAKFAST

Cool Vanilla Latte

BEVERAGE INDUSTRY PEOPLE DON'T TEND TO BE morning people, and Jerri Banks is no exception. Ms. Banks, a consultant to restaurants, was polite and informative on the telephone Thursday morning, but the call woke her up, as she warmed to her subject, like a cup of spiked coffee.

We were talking about flavored spirits, an idea that the liquor industry can't seem to get enough of. Was it light-years ago or the 1980s that Stolichnaya's "pepper" vodkas, now back on the far edge of the universe, were introduced, followed by the groves of citruses like Absolut's Citron?

This month, to name a few, Skyy vodka is unveiling Spiced Berry and Vanilla. Stolichnaya is adding Cranberi and Citros to its Ohranji, Strasberi, Razberi, Vanil and Persik (peach). And Bacardi joins the party with Razz, Cóco and Vaníla rums, making five flavors—the originals are Limón and O—in its line.

Ms. Banks shoots from the hip, a.m. or otherwise.

"Less than half of them are well done," she said of the category. "It's a bit of pie in the sky—hopefully to get a new product out and be a wild success. The market is creating a frenzy."

The news got uglier.

"Look at who orders the flavors," Ms. Banks said, confirming a cynical question about who the industry thought it was cornering. "The larger portion who order flavors—by name and by brand—are women."

Ms. Banks, whose business is four years old, has worked in the hospitality industry since the 1970s "in every position—bartender, waiter, manager—you can imagine," she said, and she knows what attitudes are. ("It was just as restaurants were making the shift to having more mixed staffs, not just women working coffee shops and diners," Ms. Banks recalled.)

There are also flavored spirits out there that get as close to the natural source of the flavor as you get to a lemon in a tree. And there are flavors, as sly as genies, that will never be bottled, Ms. Banks said. If you ever see blueberry vodka, for example, run.

Ms. Banks developed the Cool Vanilla Latte with Bacardi's Vaníla, a kind of Starbucks-generation Irish coffee, for Lamu in Manhattan.

"I've often thought of breakfast cocktails," she said. "Do you call them breakfast 'drinks'? I think it could be a lovely drink for that.

"Because rum, unlike vodka, has a flavor of its own, a slight spicy quality and a sweeter base, it melds better with flavors," she explained.

Ms. Banks's first rule of the road: test a flavored spirit on its own merits, or don't mix with it.

"The merit of a good liquor is that it stand alone, which many flavored spirits don't feel required to do," she said. "If I can't enjoy it, sipping it on ice, I don't want to use it."

Ms. Banks, tousle-haired and wearing a brown distressed-leather jacket, an untucked white dress shirt, and black slacks with black loafers when we met to drink, didn't look like a liquor's best crack at a second chance.

COOL VANILLA LATTE

ADAPTED FROM LAMU

2 ounces cool espresso
4 tablespoons milk foam
1¹/₂ ounces Bacardi Vaníla
¹/₂ ounce white crème de cacao
1 ounce skim milk
Dash of nutmeg

Pour the espresso into a chilled martini glass. Top with foam. Combine the liquor, crème de cacao and skim milk in cocktail shaker. Add ice and shake well. Strain the ingredients into a glass, pouring at the edge so as not to disturb the foam. Dust with nutmeg.

Yield: 1 serving

THE VODKA WARS

AU REVOIR AND OUT

French Martini

Dr. Kenneth Mukamal's findings were published in January 2003. The news just gets better. A study whose findings were released in March 2004 suggested that moderate drinking not only had protective cardiovascular effects, but that it was also protective for people with hypertension.

I STOPPED INTO THE RUSTIC LITTLE BAR at Fleur de Sel the other night to celebrate the Liberation—the news last week, published in a study in *The New England Journal of Medicine*, that drinking often is good for you. Dr. Kenneth Mukamal of the Harvard Medical School, who directed the study, speculated that regular, moderate drinking thins the blood, which reduces the risk of heart attack by about a third.

Thank you, Dr. Mukamal, from the bottom of my glass.

I chose a French martini to greet my freedom from worry, guilt and doubt—a drink with the pink of health. A French martini is typically a vodka martini, with the addition of Chambord Liqueur Royale de France, a black raspberry Cognac liqueur that also includes citrus, cinnamon, vanilla and French acacia honey.

It is bottled in a spherical decanter with a crown for a cap, which looks like a cross between the pope's private stock and a Haitian church altar ornament. Recalling the French Riviera more than the Sun King, Chambord is also a feature of Sex on the Beach.

Because of a soft, not a spirited edge, the French martini has a double appeal as a cocktail and as an aperitif. Variations incorporate Lillet, and a variety of fruit juices like pineapple. I have it on some authority, from a rearrived ex-pat, that the drink was popular a few years ago in Paris, on the bar row of the Rue de Lappe.

The French martini can also be served as a shooter called an adrenaline. A shooter is a shot-glass-based cocktail, meant to do business quickly. Au revoir and out.

At Fleur de Sel, a restaurant on East 20th Street, the French martini has a fan of mandolin-thin green apple slices lining the glass, as in a tart pan.

What Ratha Chau, the general manager, called a cappuccino of frothed French cider graces the drink at the surface, poured as a flourish from a second shaker.

The cocktail has a classic, if quiet taste, with a too-many-cooks quality to the presentation. I would lose the pie and the pond scum. The appearance of a drink's liquid is the sum total of its elegance in a glass, and you want to see it. The French martini is Chanel pink— don't squander opportunities like that.

I swung by a liquor store, picked up a mini orb of Chambord, headed home and tried making my own. I ramped up the vodka, to stiffen the pastel in the palate, and topped the cocktail with a splash of sparkling cider, to give it effervescence without a cloud. I left its jewel-like color to speak for itself.

It talked tough like a martini. But it was in the language of love.

FRENCH MARTINI

ADAPTED FROM FLEUR DE SEL

Thinly sliced green apples
Pinch of fleur de sel
1 ounce vodka
$^1/_4$ ounce Chambord Liqueur Royale de France
Splash of pineapple juice
Splash of apple cider

Line the martini glass with sliced green apples, with the skins dusted with fleur de sel. Mix the vodka, Chambord and juice in a shaker with ice; chill and strain into glass. Shake the cider till it foams and pour on top.

Yield: 1 serving

THAT'S WHAT VODKA'S FOR

Red Lemon

Arnold Schwarzenegger, the Austrian-born actor, was sworn in as the thirty-eighth governor of California in November 2003.

SPEAKING OF AUSTRIANS AT A FUNNY POINT IN THEIR careers, there's Red Bull, the nonalcoholic energy drink. It is produced in Austria and was introduced in the United States in 1997; a billion cans were sold globally last year.

But it is as an ingredient in cocktails, not as a gym buzz, that Red Bull gets interesting. Initially insiders on the late-night circuit of D.J.s and their bicoastal, after-party ilk, Red Bull cocktails are now cresting in popularity across the country—a great inland wave. What was a novelty is today an order in any bar.

Red Bull and vodka is Generation Y's gin and tonic, a genuinely original cocktail for the twenty-first century. The partnership has its own Web pages such as *VodkaRed* (www.vrfan.barbiehead.org). People under twenty-five are making it history.

When Tyler Peyton and his partners opened Lit in Oklahoma City last year, intent on making the nightclub the epicenter of the local scene, they understood that they had to offer Red Bull. Mr. Peyton, twenty-five, created an exclusive section for it on the cocktail list, which includes the Red Lemon, the Fuzzy Bull and the

Red-Headed Slut, which includes Jagermeiser, peach schnapps and cranberry juice.

"There are about sixty-plus cocktails known," he said last week. "The weirdest one I've seen is Red Bull and Guinness."

Mr. Peyton explained, "It's the 'in' thing. And everyone wants to do the 'in' thing, especially in this town." Lit's bar goes through twenty 24-can cases of Red Bull a week. "It's younger people," Mr. Peyton said of the Red Bull drinkers' base. "We've tried it on older people—forty-plus. They're probably up until four in the morning."

It's not how Red Bull tastes in a cocktail. Loaded with caffeine (where did *you* think energy came from?), it's what Red Bull with liquor does. It is the echo boomer's Frisco speedball.

"It kind of wakes you up," Mr. Peyton said. "You're still loose, but energetic and you have fun. It gets you going for a good night."

Red Bull and vodka has been called Ecstasy in a can, a reference to a popular club drug. It has also had its run-in with the law: the drink was briefly investigated in 2001 by the Swedish National Food Administration after the deaths of three people who were believed to have drunk Red Bull with liquor. No action was taken against the company, Red Bull GmbH. The drink continues to be available in Sweden and in eighty-eight other countries.

"It's for sale in clubs and bars, but we don't promote it as a mixer," said a spokesman for Red Bull North America on Thursday. "It's a phenomenon that happened on its own."

One thing that everyone will agree on is that it's almost impossible to describe the taste. Mixed with Bacardi Limon in a Red Lemon, Red Bull tastes like an energy Chartreuse: herbal and sweet, with acidity and slight carbonation. Or, a cough drop from hell.

"I don't know how to describe it—it's a little medicinal," said Stefan Trummer, who with his brother Albert enjoys renown in New York as a celebrity bartender, or "bar chef." The Trummers are Austrian.

Mr. Trummer grew up drinking Red Bull, but it has confounded him as a bar chef.

"I tried to make a couple of specialty drinks—with Champagne, as a sorbet—but nothing really satisfied me," he said.

Mr. Trummer, that's what vodka's for.

RED LEMON

2 ounces Bacardi Limon
2 ounces Red Bull

Mix the ingredients together in a mixing glass. Serve over ice in an old-fashioned glass.

Yield: 1 serving

THE TIME-SPACE CONTINUUM

Cosmic Cocktail

The Massachusetts Supreme Judicial Court ruled in November 2003 that it was unconstitutional to deny marriage licenses to same-sex couples, staying its decision for 180 days. On May 17, 2004, same-sex marriage became legal in Massachusetts, the first state to recognize it.

IS THERE GAY MARRIAGE ON OTHER PLANETS?
I was pondering this one evening while I stood at the entrance to the Rose Center for Earth and Space on West 81st Street at the American Museum of Natural History. There was a cocktail party in progress in the exhibition hall below the sphere of the Hayden Planetarium, and I watched it as I waited for a guest. *House and Garden* magazine was celebrating itself and its March issue, which was a celebration of color, and the evening was also a fund-raising event for DIFFA, or the Design Industries Foundation Fighting AIDS.

Theatrical lights with colored gels projected party-colored Champagne bubbles onto the bottom of the Planetarium, and fog machines rolled fog out onto the floor. Waiters stood at the sides, like a clone army, holding trays of cocktails. A large multipaneled television screen played promotional spots for *House and Garden*, Pantone and Jeep—the party's sponsors. I thought Jeep commercials were a little terrestrial, given the venue, but nobody drinking the cocktails or eating the mini hamburgers seemed to be paying much attention to the screen. The music was "groovy" rock, and Nancy Sinatra singing "Boots" was *House and Garden*'s idea of the edge of the known universe.

From the balcony in the Rose Center's blue-lighted lobby, the scene looked like a party in a *Batman* movie, Gotham, not New York, as though New Yorkers had decided it was easier to accept self-parody and enjoy it than to fight it, and I felt the want of face paint and costumes until a man showed up behind me at the registry desk wearing a black ski cap, a white tunic and a white cape with a peace sign on the back, constructed from sequins. The *House and Garden* invitation read: "Attire—Whatever On Earth." He'll do.

But the Rose Center, in its labeled displays, posed disturbing questions that I feared the answers to: things about "Intelligent Life," etc.

Manhattan is the mothership of several species that wouldn't well survive outside of it. Photo stylists, decorators' assistants, creative directors, ad sales reps. What would a visitor to the planet make of a *House and Garden* party? Do other star systems have magazines? Magazines that publish commentary like "Simply Chic!" or "Ralph Lauren's Instant Classic"? Is an instant classic the result of the time-space continuum?

My guest arrived, and we went in.

Like most events in New York now, the party boasted its own specialty cocktail. It was a Cosmic Cocktail, which is a cosmopolitan with pomegranate juice. Pomegranate was the "it" fruit juice of 2003, mostly due to the promotional efforts of a California pomegranate producer who introduced POM Wonderful, a bottled juice, nationally in 2003. A pomegranate martini developed by Dale DeGroff, the ex–Rainbow Room bartender and the "King of Cocktails," was the official cocktail of the 2004 Academy Awards Governor's Ball.

Mayer Rus, *House and Garden*'s design editor, dutifully stepped up onto the wagon, and pronounced the pomegranate the "Fruit of the Year" in his back-page column in the March 2004 issue—handily hoisting the pomegranate into the pantheon of punch-makers (an instant classic!) just in time for the party.

I picked a pomegranate from a tree once, on Stromboli, an island in the Tyrrhenian Sea, off the coast of Italy. It looked like something from another planet, especially when you cut it open—a seed pod from another world. A world, like Stromboli, where you watch silver anchovies leap in silver schools from the sea, or converse with a mule tied under a tree, who will bray at you indulgently for hours, content with your company, or where you wait on a rough stone step for the grocer to come back from lunch, to buy your food for dinner.

Regretfully, that world is our own, I reflected sadly at the Rose Center that night, only rarely.

COSMIC COCKTAIL

ADAPTED FROM *HOUSE AND GARDEN*

2 ounces vodka
3 ounces pomegranate juice
1 ounce triple sec
Dash of fresh lime juice or Rose's Lime Juice
Purple sugar

Shake all the ingredients, except sugar, with ice. Strain into a chilled martini glass that has been rimmed in sugar. (Wet the rim by wiping it with a lime wedge, then dip the glass lightly onto a plate of sugar.)

Yield: 1 serving

THE NEW KID

Town Plum

Cîroc was introduced in 2003: the category, and competition, continues to grow, as vodka holds its lead in the spirits industry.

THERE'S NOTHING LIKE BEING THE NEW KID IN TOWN.

Cîroc, a French vodka made from grapes—what else?—was introduced in the New York area two weeks ago, after opening out of town in Chicago. Two years in development, it was created for the United States market, and may find its way back to France eventually if it sells well here.

The new vodka rode in on a carefully orchestrated drumbeat of buzz, hype and plain old publicity, which began in February. By the time Cîroc appeared in A-list restaurants like the Four Seasons, B-plus bars like Randy Gerber's Whiskey chain and suburban liquor stores like Hewlett Wine and Liquors, in Hewlett, New York, the media kits with the silver-plated key chains, and the complimentary cases to Hollywood agents, had gone out, and Bill Clinton and Jennifer Aniston had been spotted drinking it (though not with arms entwined) in the gossip columns. Then it went on sale—one 80 proof degree of separation from Mrs. Brad Pitt and the forty-second president—at a suggested $29.99 for a 750-milliliter bottle.

The super-premium, or "ultra-premium," vodka category, as

Cîroc's brand manager, Efren Puente, called it, is a growth business for an otherwise stagnant liquor industry. The category was up more than 40 percent in sales last year, and the increase has bred nothing but hope for fresh faces.

Absolut redefined vodka in the 1980s as a premium drink. The field is being redefined again by brands like Grey Goose, Chopin and Belvedere—the big-gun super-premiums. Add recently arrived Mor and Ston from Estonia and Zyr and Charodei from Russia, and you have enough ex-Communist-bloc players to make a pornographic film.

Cîroc has the standard "ultra-premium" kit—unique bottle and interminable story. "Snap frost" grapes, small village in southwestern France, cold fermenting, distilled five times (the previous record for super-premiums appears to be four). The "Rollerball" trophy bottle was designed by Gordon Smith, an industrial designer in London who also designed Tanqueray No. Ten gin.

"There were a great many frosted bottles," Mr. Smith said of his research with focus groups. "Consumers were clued in to this, and asked, 'Please don't give us another frosted bottle.'" Cîroc's bottle uses "a particular silica, which gives super-clarity," Mr. Smith said.

"Drink is one of the most active markets in the world," he added of designing a "sell" like vodka. "It's continually moving, and changing itself. And every single country in the world has a product which is alcohol based. It's fascinating for a designer."

Does Cîroc taste different? James Moreland, the bar chef at Town Bar on West 56th Street in New York, is specifying it in a new cocktail, the Town Plum, to be included on his menu in April, not because of its advance men, he said, but its flavor. (Mr. Moreland recommends Polish bison-grass vodka for apple martinis, for example.)

"Vodka is the most difficult of them all to try to sort out, because there are just so many of them," Mr. Moreland said. "Some are marketing gigs—'Who's got the prettiest bottle?' You have to pick a vodka that will complement your flavors, or mixes well with the season's ingredients."

Cîroc has been assigned to Mr. Moreland's top shelf, a Valhalla of vodkas. Charbay, a five-year-old California vodka, came down to make room for it.

You're only as good as your last cocktail, kid.

TOWN PLUM

ADAPTED FROM TOWN BAR

1 1/2 ounces Cîroc grape vodka
3/4 ounce plum nectar
Juice of 1/4 lime
Juice of 1/4 lemon
A few purple grapes

Strain the liquid ingredients and shake lightly with ice. Pour into a deep tumbler. Garnish with grapes sliced in half. Stir.

Yield: 1 serving

TWO LOUNGERS

LIQUIDITY

Apple Martini

PETER MESKOURIS IS CLEARLY A LADIES' MAN. Mr. Meskouris, twenty-seven, stood at his bar at H.K. at 523 Ninth Avenue last Sunday afternoon, talking with a pair of patrons: young women, one age twenty-four and the other "six months older," as her friend explained, each wearing spaghetti-strap tank tops that revealed tiny, delicate tattoos.

Mr. Meskouris, a smooth, solid man who wears a diamond stud in each ear and has impeccably barbered eyebrows, invited them to his New Year's Eve party. The restaurant would be closed but open to "friends and people we know," he said. The women sipped at the small straws in their Collins glasses—which didn't sound like a "no."

But business is business. And Mr. Meskouris has business on his mind. H.K., which stands for Hell's Kitchen, is two weeks old. And Mr. Meskouris, his brother Alex and a cousin, Peter, scions of the Jackson Hole burger-joint enterprise, a family operation that includes nine restaurants, are $700,000 lighter. After ten months of renovation, the three, who grew up together, have jointly opened H.K., a former bodega, above which Mr. Meskouris used to live. He said he started saving money for his own restaurant when he was thirteen, working for his father at Jackson Hole. The apartment upstairs is now a convenient couch and a shower for twelve- to eighteen-hour days below.

Mr. Meskouris designed H.K., its menu and its drinks list, and he has adhered to the new cocktail bar, lounge and restaurant formula lethally, as only a twenty-seven-year-old could. The dining room is twenty-first-century diner style: industrial steel and gloss white, with a roll-up garage door that opens the restaurant to the street. Three flat-screen televisions electronically billboard the top of the bar. The menu is sun-dried, roasted and grilled. And the drinks list has a page of martinis, a page of specialty cocktails, forty-five vodkas (including flavors), eighteen tequilas and seven single-barrel bourbons. It reads like a wine list.

Martinis include the most popular martinis that are not martinis to purists, like the reigning princess of the problem, the apple martini. Mr. Meskouris has two, apple and sour apple.

It's 2004, and the apple martini is here to stay. It's not a gin martini, but it's not a bad drink. It's tart when it should be sweet, and it presents well. It has a crisp, pale-cash liquidity that makes it look as if it's enjoyable to spend. Every cocktail is a charge against your time, and you learn quickly what not to order. Mr. Meskouris makes his apple martini with Berentzen's apple liqueur, a pricey schnapps that gives it a platinum edge.

Mr. Meskouris also managed the construction on H.K., down to the last square foot of concrete flooring. Last Sunday, living on the nerve energy of a new restaurateur, he insisted on a tour of the women's bathroom, which was beautiful. There was a place for a small sofa and good lighting above the mirrors.

A ladies' man clearly had a hand in it.

APPLE MARTINI

ADAPTED FROM H.K.

5 ounces vodka
2 ounces Berentzen apple liqueur
1 ounce Midori melon liqueur
Green apple slice

Combine the liquid ingredients in a shaker with ice. Shake until chilled, then strain into an 8-ounce martini glass and garnish with apple.

Yield: 1 serving

HEY, YOU

The Stone Rose

The $1.7-billion, 2.8-million-square-foot Time Warner Center opened in February 2004, after seven years in construction. Jewel and Marc Anthony performed at the opening-night party. Five thousand apple martinis awaited arriving guests.

THE NEW TIME WARNER CENTER AT COLUMBUS CIRCLE, being basically a late-model shopping mall, had to have one of each and the "lounge," or the exciting nightlife space, is Stone Rose Lounge, on the fourth floor.

The 6,500-square-foot Stone Rose is Rande Gerber's. Mr. Gerber is the creator of the Whiskey chain, which was a successful franchise for Ian Schrager's Paramount on West 45th Street, one of the original boutique hotels. The Whiskey bars are now based in W hotels across the country and in Mexico City. Mr. Gerber is also, famously, Mr. Cindy Crawford.

Maybe in a defensive nod to the idea that Rockefeller Center, the Midtown jewel of Manhattan, is also basically a shopping mall, albeit a legendary one, Mr. Gerber and his designers, Yabu Pushelberg, have styled the soaring Stone Rose in the image of a classic Art Deco interior, with rosewood-paneled walls and red mirrors and leather-clad columns. The bar is rosewood topped, with a stitched-leather edge. The Stone Rose is clearly trying to be a hipster's Rainbow Room, the famous sky-nest restaurant and club at Rockefeller Center. It's got a wall of tall windows and a nice view of Columbus Circle, but it's not the Buck Rogers metropolis aerial that the Rainbow Room is on a black cloudless night.

The press materials that went out on Stone Rose said that the intent of its look was to "smell like money." It went on to say that it would "echo the posh atmosphere of a classically timeless hotel lounge," and it's true, the Stone Rose, more than the next Rainbow Room, could be a hotel bar in a new upscale hotel, perhaps in Hawaii.

It also has a "back door," a cherished and time-honored notion on the New York nightlife scene. But, this is the Time Warner Center, and apparently everybody is happy to use the escalators or elevators, celebrities and would-be celebrities included.

"There is another way," Mr. Gerber said, almost nostalgically, it seemed, speaking from Los Angeles where he and Ms. Crawford live. "But nobody has asked us about it."

Mr. Gerber, whose Whiskey bar at the Paramount was in its heyday in the early 1990s a strictly velvet-rope, models-meet-young-money scene, issued a statement about Stone Rose which explained that it would be "a bit more sophisticated and elegant, while still maintaining a chic and sexy lounge that our guests expect from us."

Read: broader client base. A loungeteria for the Center. You don't want to discourage shoppers from making an evening of it with a seven o'clock nightcap after a long day of pulling the plastic out of its holster. There is a standard posse of hosts at the door, beautiful blondes and well-groomed black men wearing headsets, but they could be welcoming you to the NBC television studio at Rockefeller Center for a taping of *Conan O'Brien*. This is, in a peculiar first for New York, a "theme lounge." The Stone Rose looks and acts like a New York establishment, opening somewhere else. Now that the clerks at the Gap have headsets, isn't it time to retire them?

On Tuesday, what you might expect is what you got—a big-budget, hard to get into place that was brilliantly easy to get into. It's tough being exclusive with 135 seats and a forty-five-foot-long bar. With a fourteen-foot-tall red glass sculptural screen at the entrance, like a super-size awards trophy, theatrically ushering patrons in, the

Stone Rose could be a set—the Grammys from 1994 (Record of the Year: "All I Wanna Do," by Sheryl Crow; Album of the Year: *MTV Unplugged*, by Tony Bennett).

A young pretty man with a samurai's ponytail and a British accent from somewhere in the world sat at the bar drinking an orange drink and talking to a bar waitress in a short black dress with a martini-glass-shaped cleavage that squeezed her breasts tightly up toward the Stone Rose's eighteen-foot-high ceiling.

"Are you afraid of rejection?" she asked him, then answered for him. "You're gorgeous."

The junior samurai seemed to take the observation well, arguing a little about how shy he was.

"Women flirt, too," the waitress added, explaining American ways.

The bartender was stock-item handsome and his trousers suggested he had been hired on the strength of his buttocks, which could have been selling collapsible gyms on cable television. He was serious, too, transacting business in his best audition voice—deep, with a trace of questioning to it.

"The Stone Rose," I said, handing him the menu like a script.

"The Stone Rose," he said, looking me in the eye. Take 1.

The Stone Rose cocktail is a perfectly respectable bourbon drink. It's on the sweet side, but bourbon stands up to a lot. It's the best of the bunch on the house specialty list. The Perfect Lady is perfectly innocuous, everything and nothing in taste. There's gin in there, the menu says, but it's just one pair of legs in the limo. Let's hope the Tenacious isn't. It's perfectly awful.

There seems to be a revival going on of the early Meg Ryan, now that Ms. Ryan has moved on from sleeplessness in age, hair color and, arguably, range. The blond bob, the impetuous dazzling dopey grin, the wide wide eyes, the coat-snagging friendliness. My waitress was a book-clerk bombshell, a romantic comedy waiting to happen.

"Hey, you," she said, confronting me with my drink as though it might change my life. "Why are you taking notes?"

"Because," I began, in my best honk of a Hanks, "I want to remember this moment forever."

THE STONE ROSE

1¹/₂ ounces Woodford Reserve Bourbon
¹/₂ ounce Grand Marnier
1 ounce white cranberry juice
Splash of sour mix *(see Note)*
Splash of simple syrup
Maraschino cherry

Shake the ingredients, except the cherry, vigorously with ice. Strain into a chilled martini glass and garnish with a cherry.

Yield: 1 serving

Note: The Stone Rose Lounge makes its own sour mix, which is a ratio of the juice of one freshly squeezed lemon to one freshly squeezed lime, with sugar and water added to taste.

INDEX BY MAIN LIQUOR